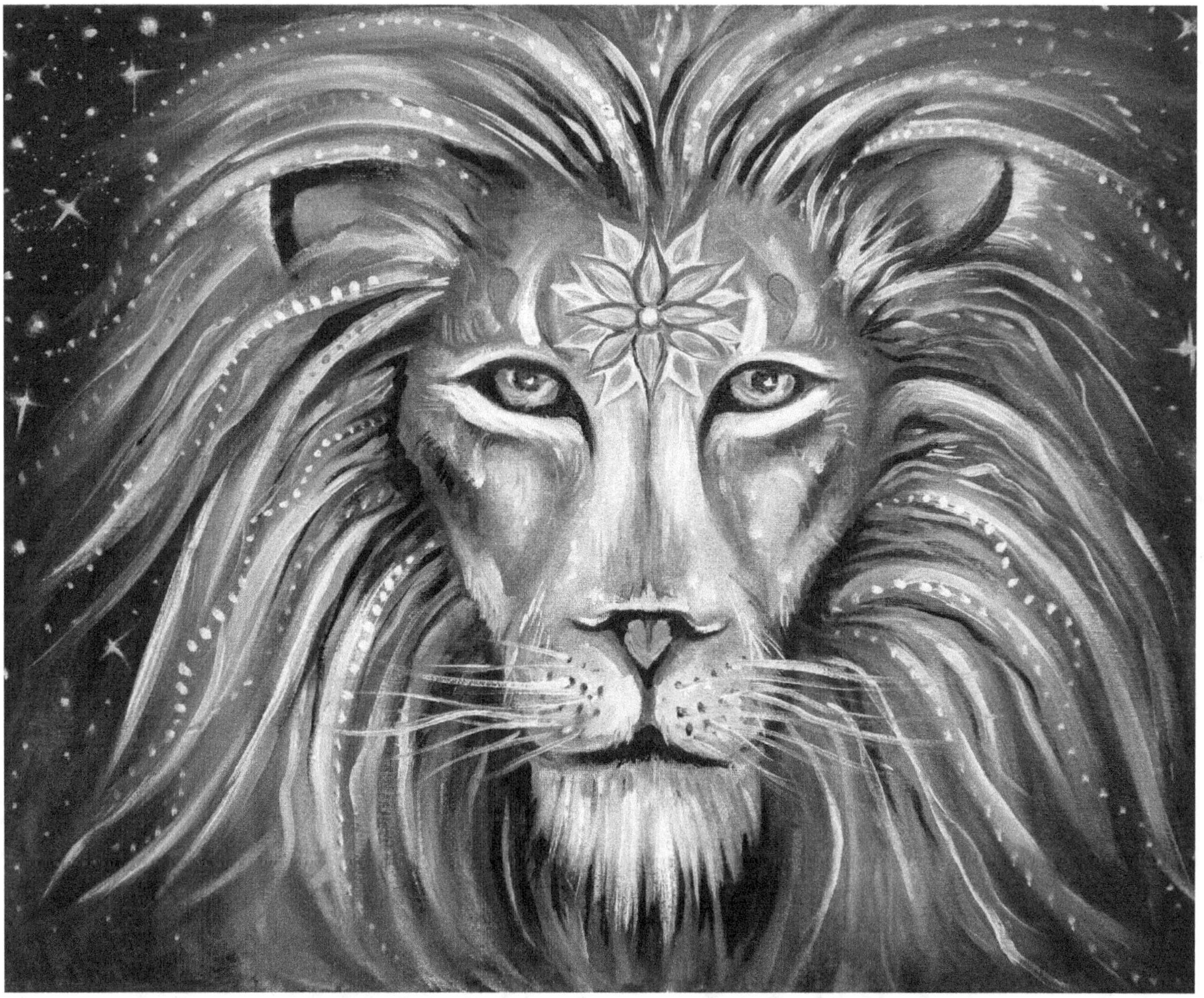

DEDICATED

To the heartbeat of my life,
my dear (wife)

And to my sun and moon,
(Noor and Farah)

You are the inspiration
and joy of every day.

This book is the
fruit of the love
you've planted in
my heart,

And I hope it brings
every child the happiness
that you fill my life with.

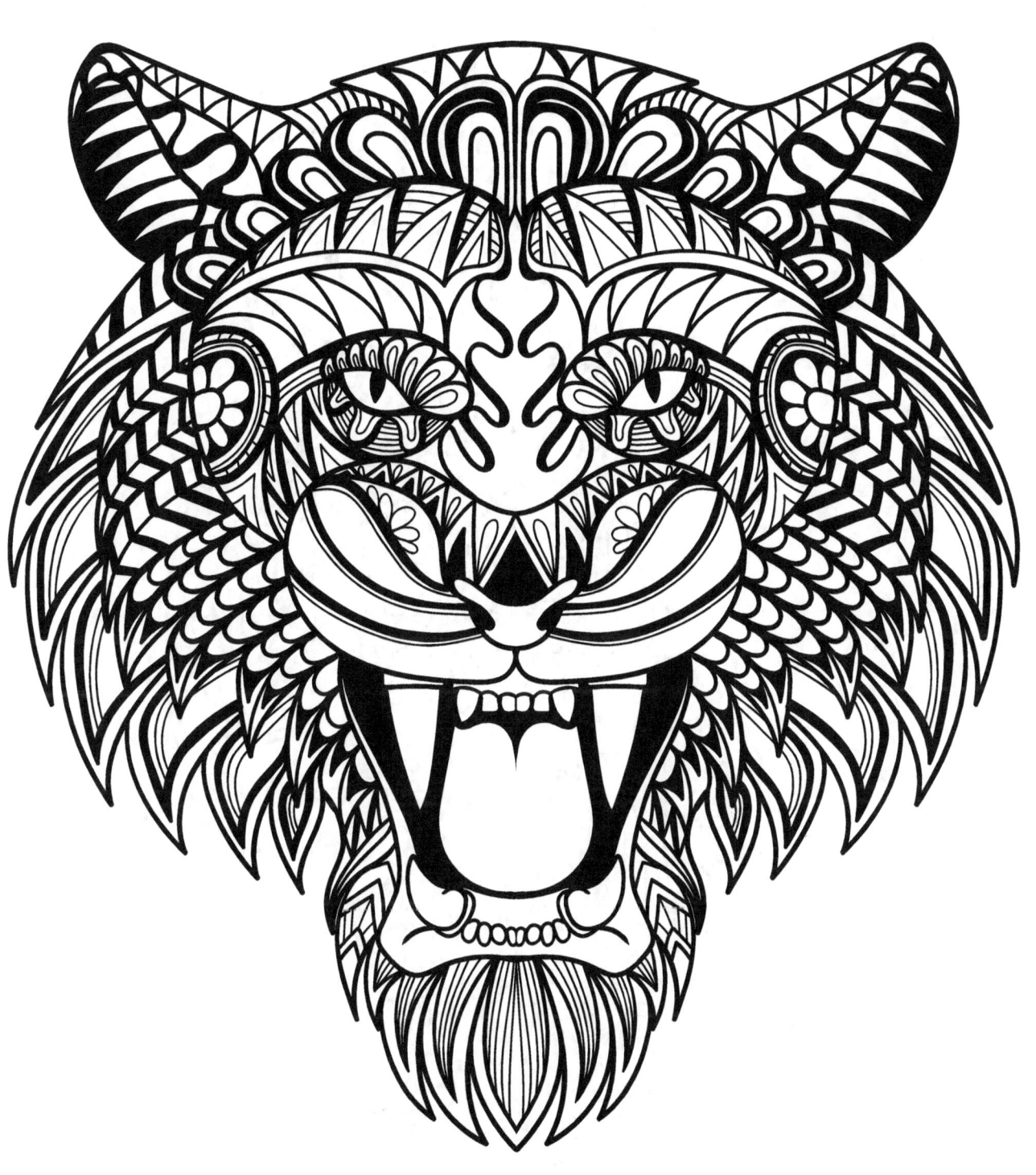

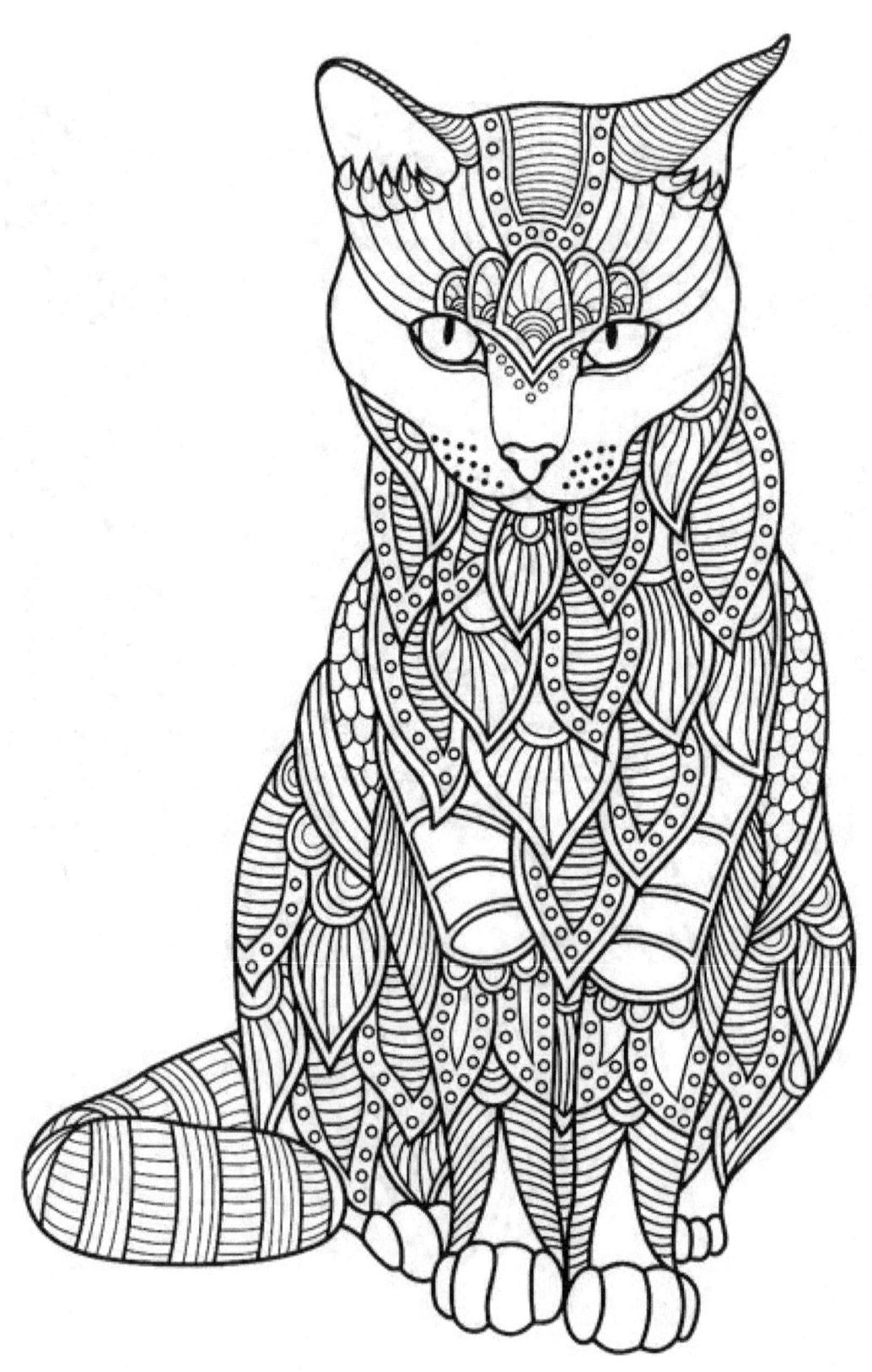

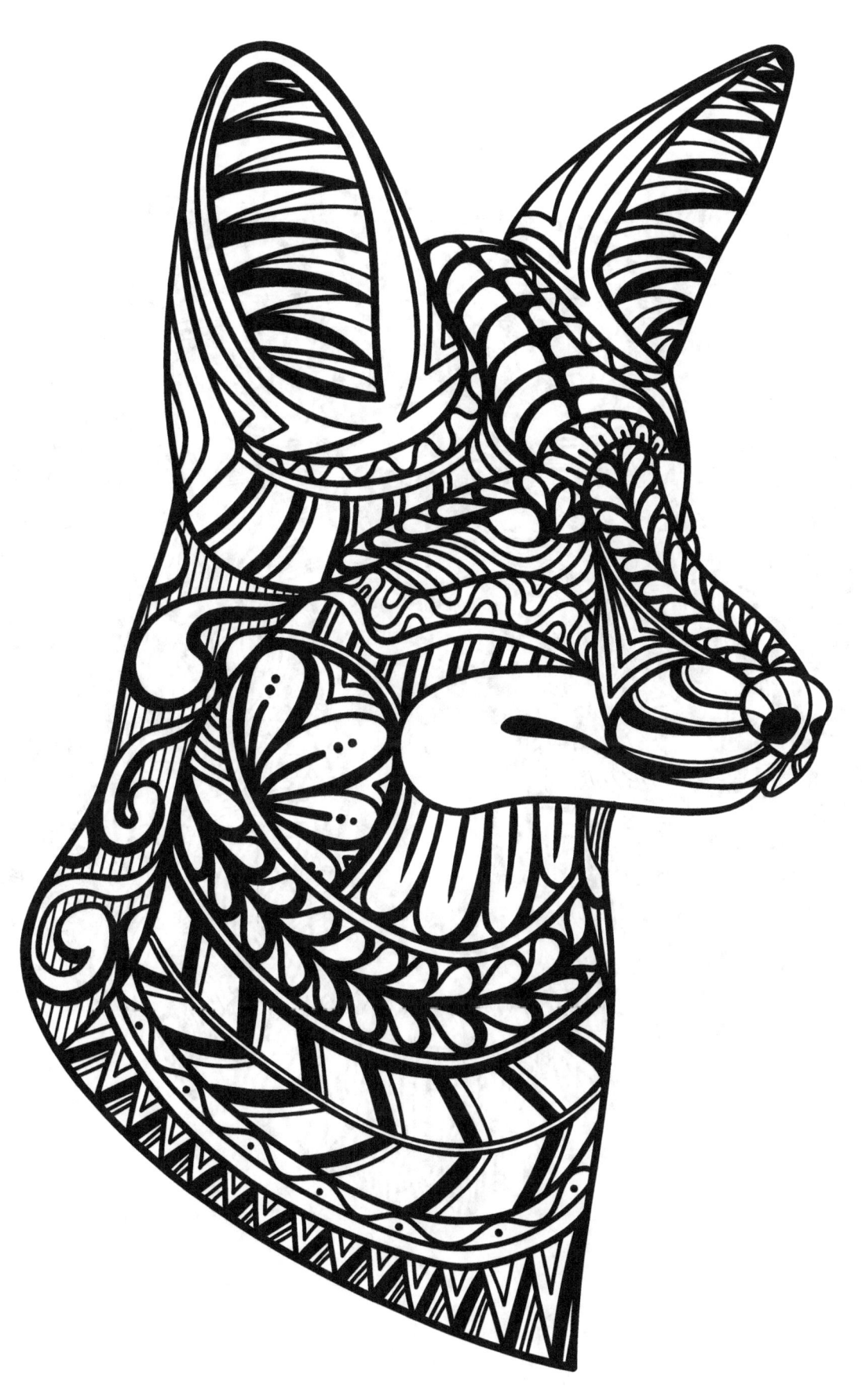

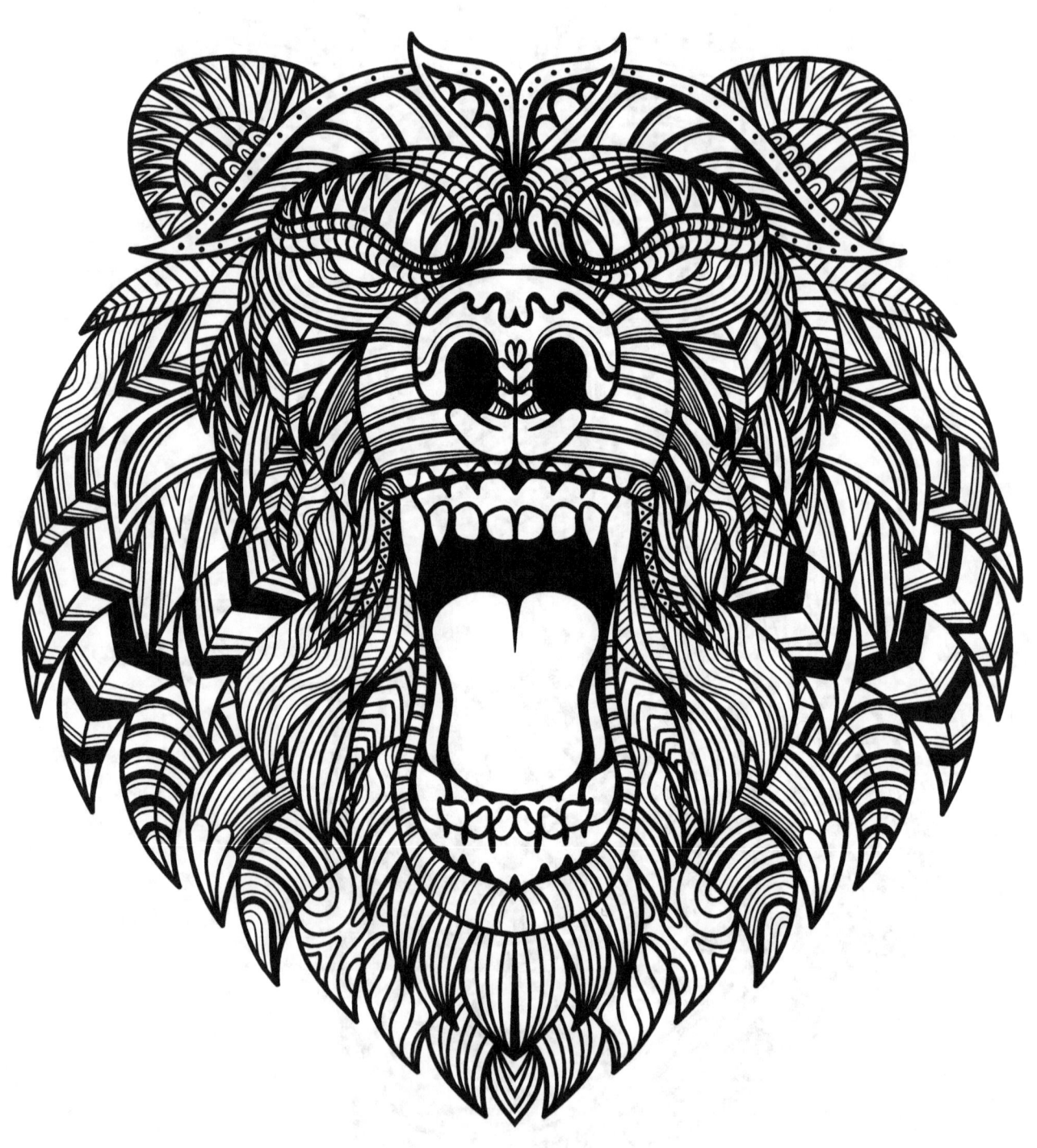

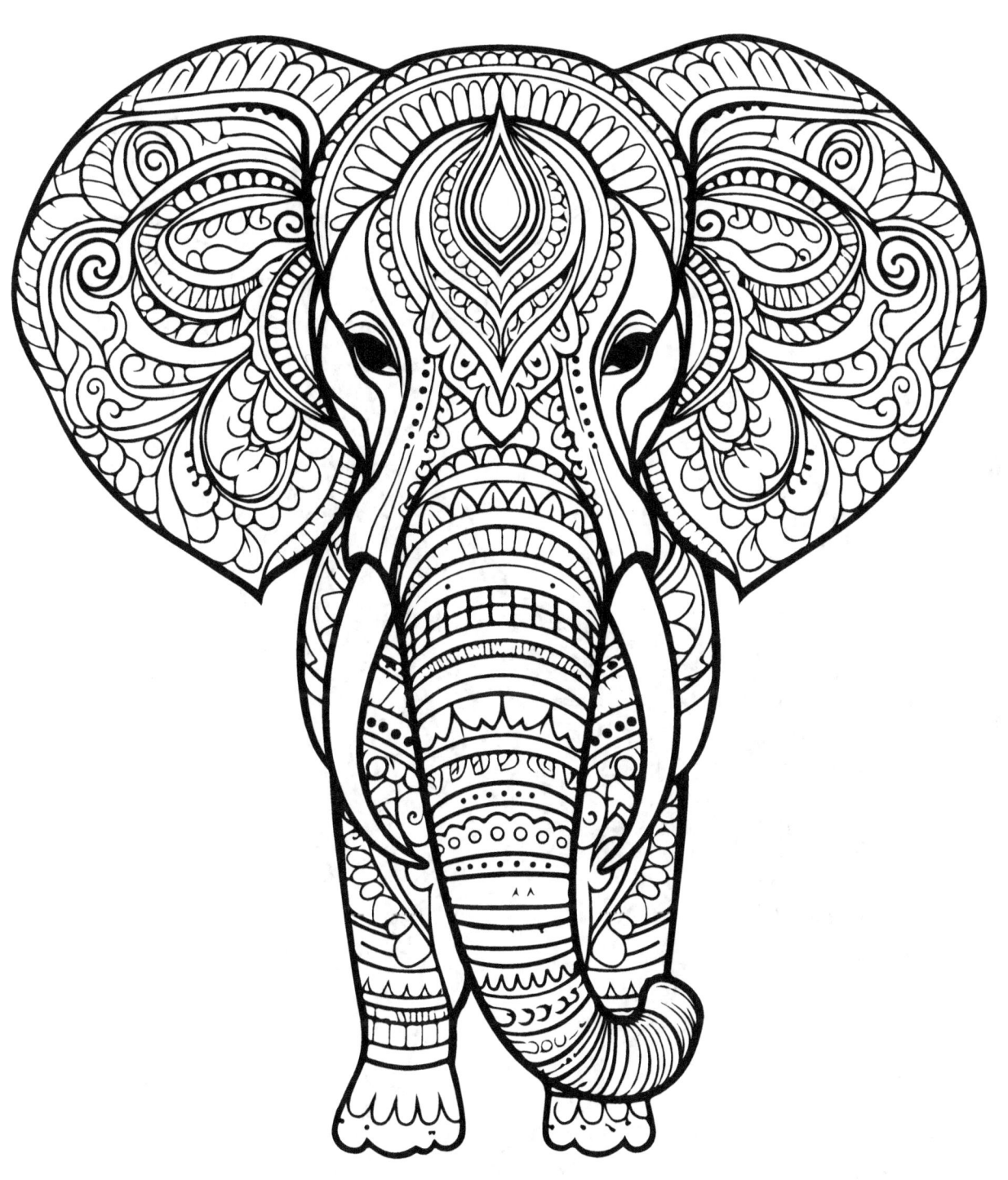

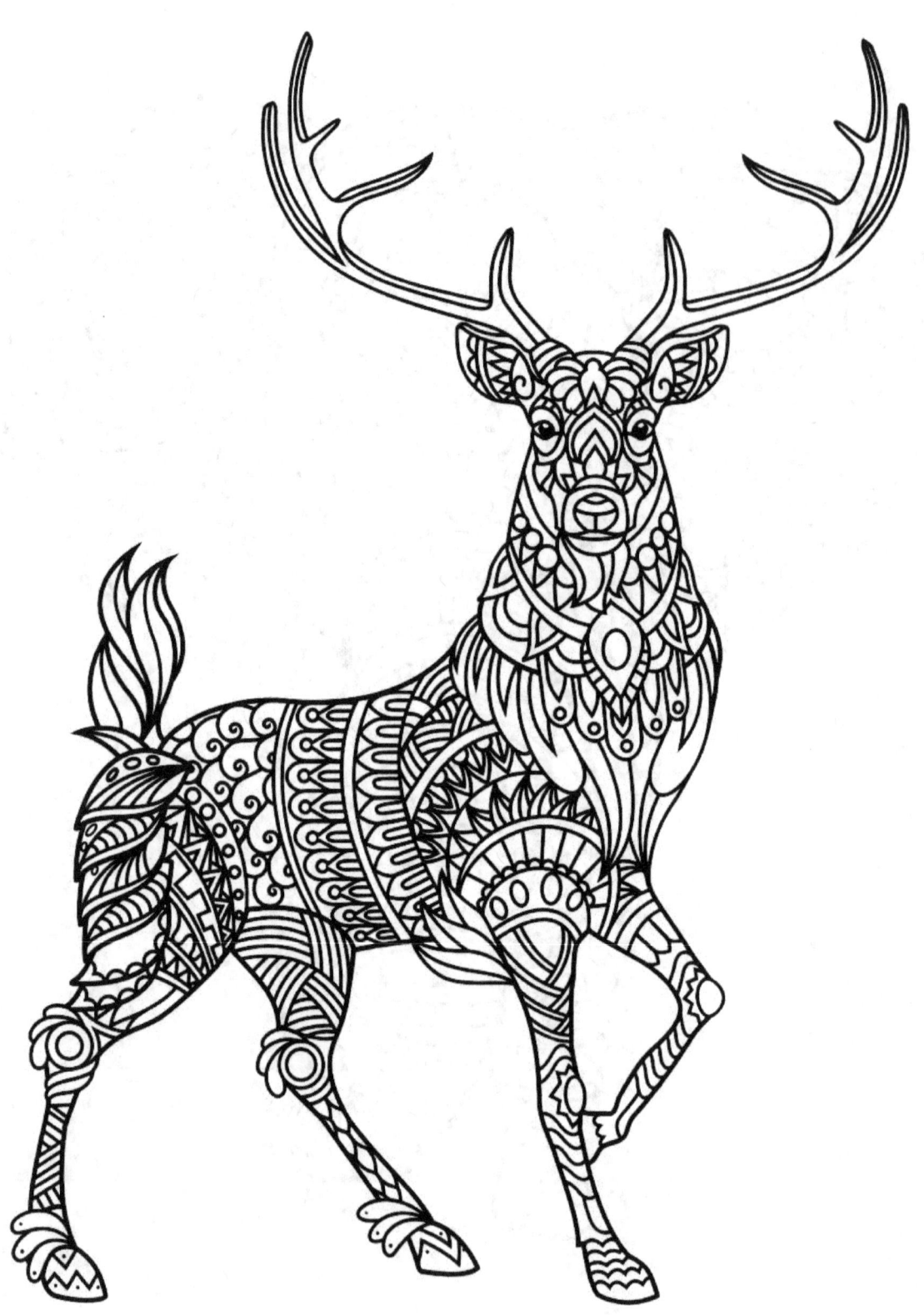

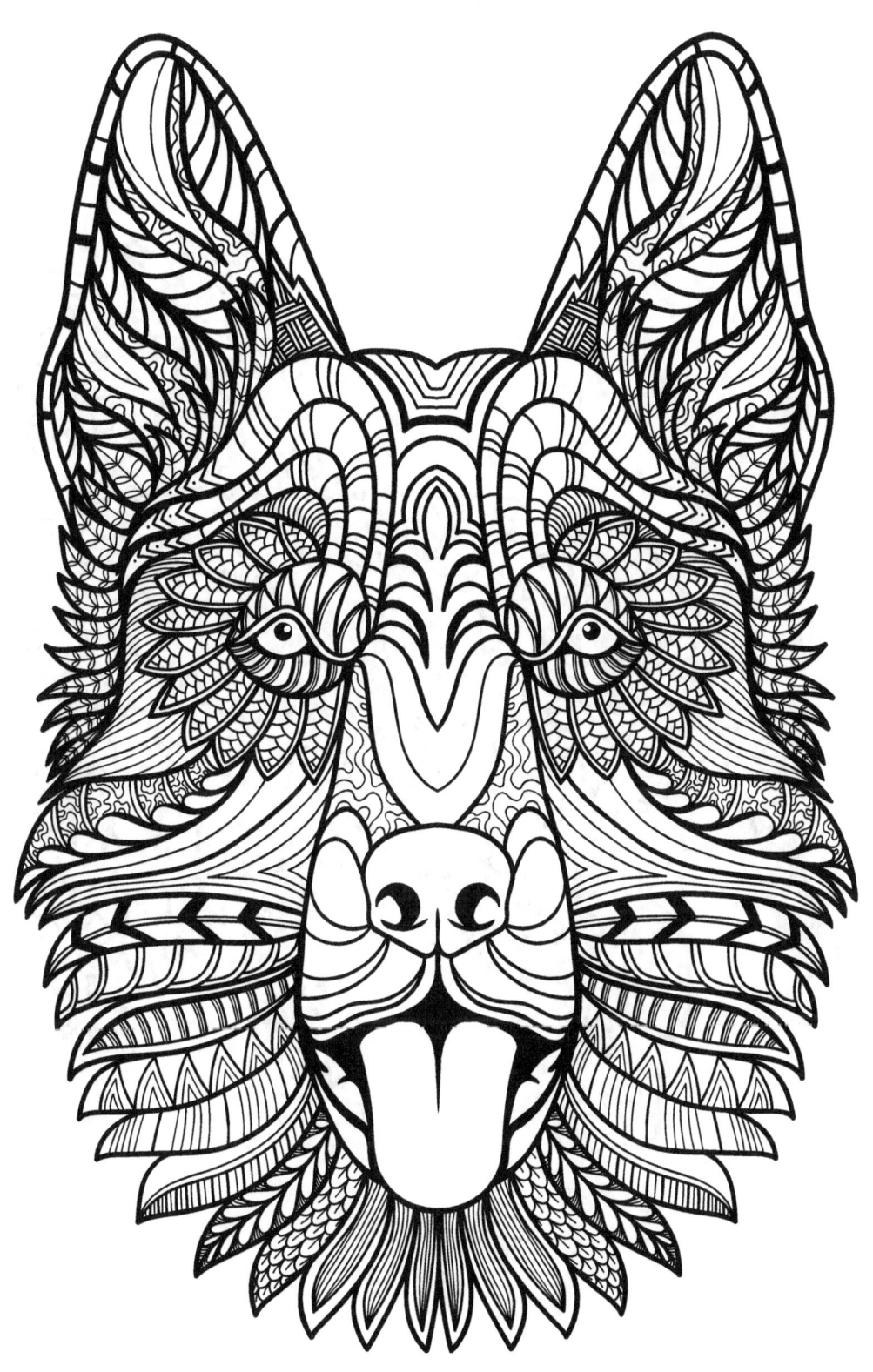

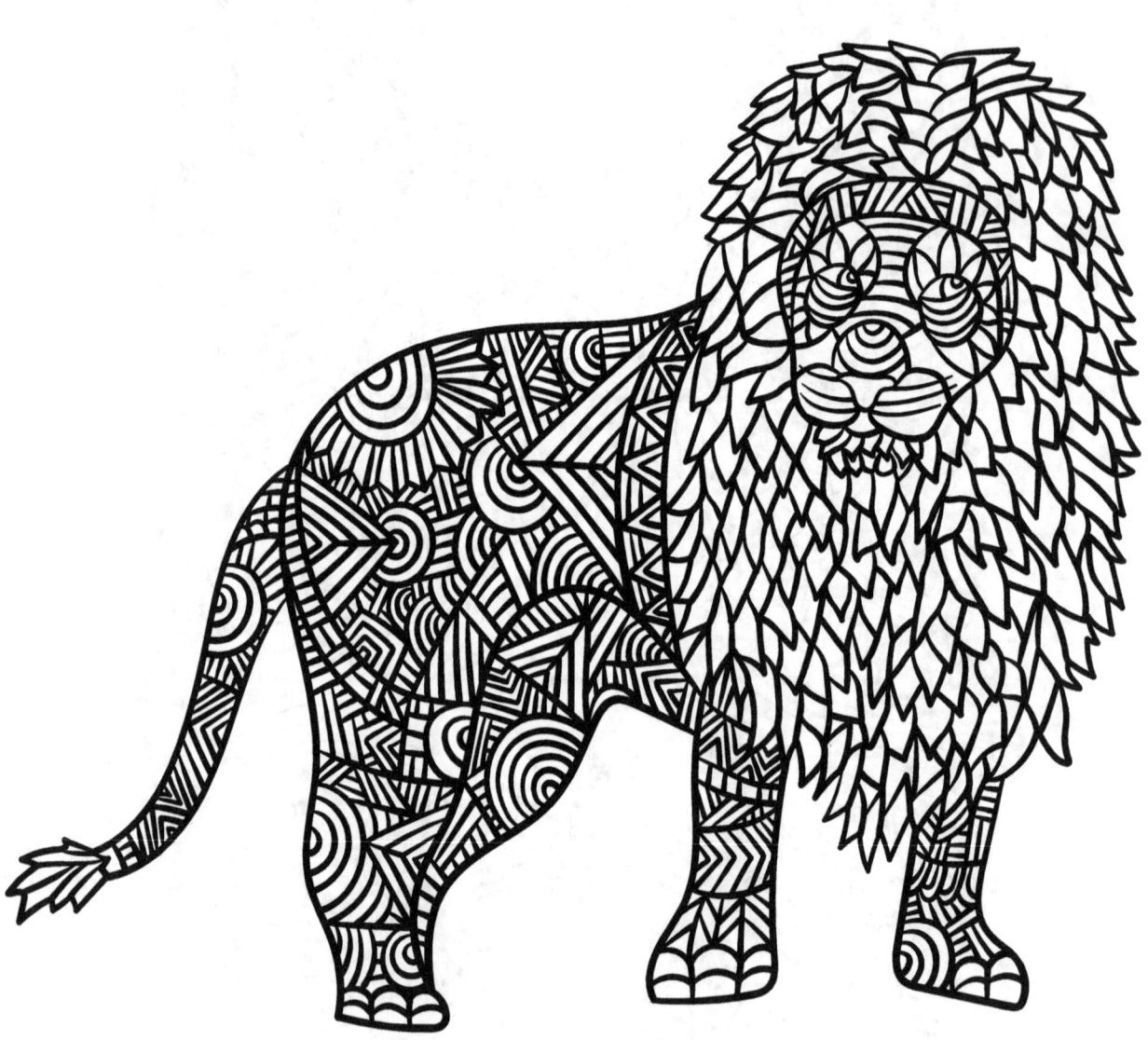

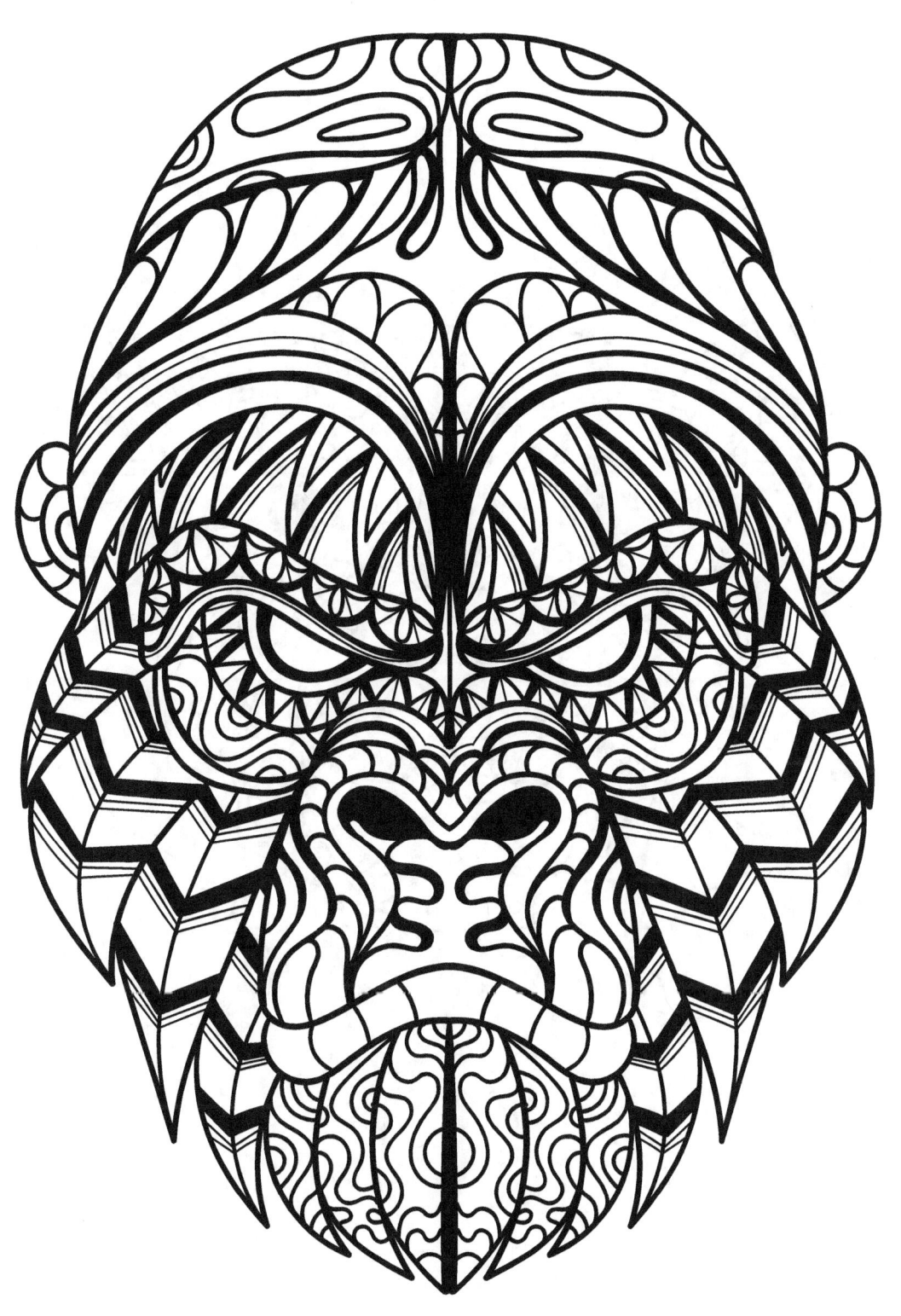

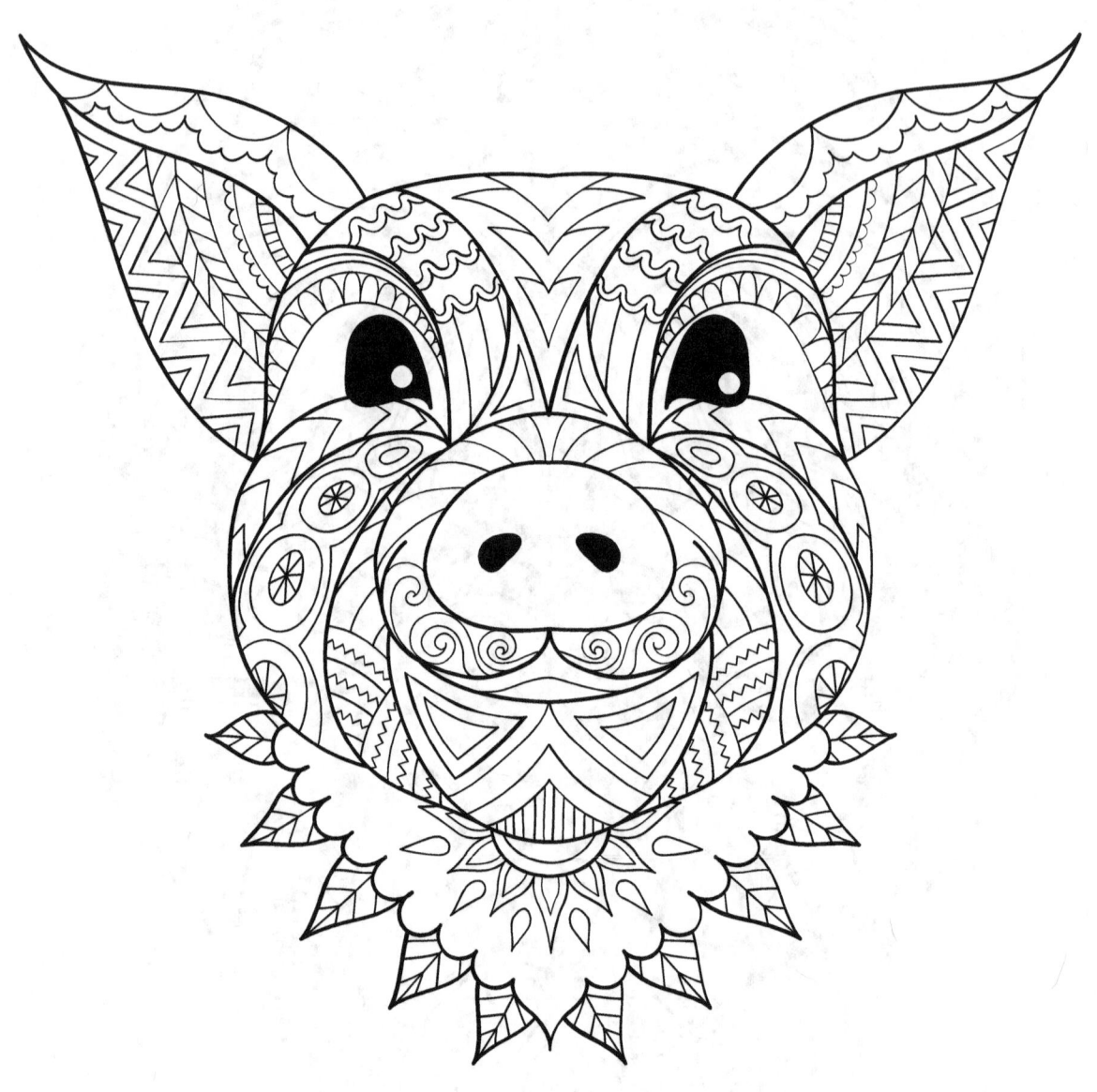

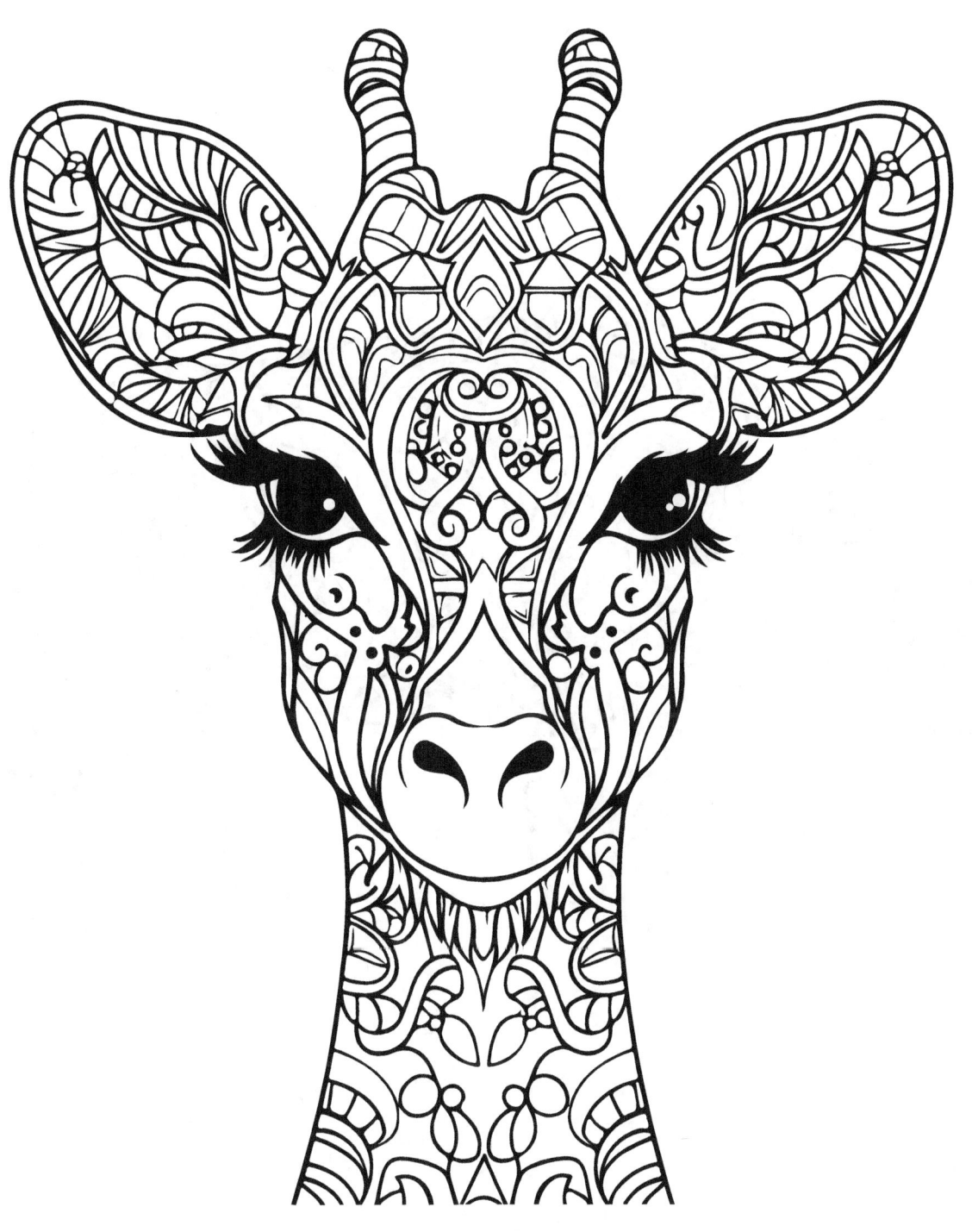

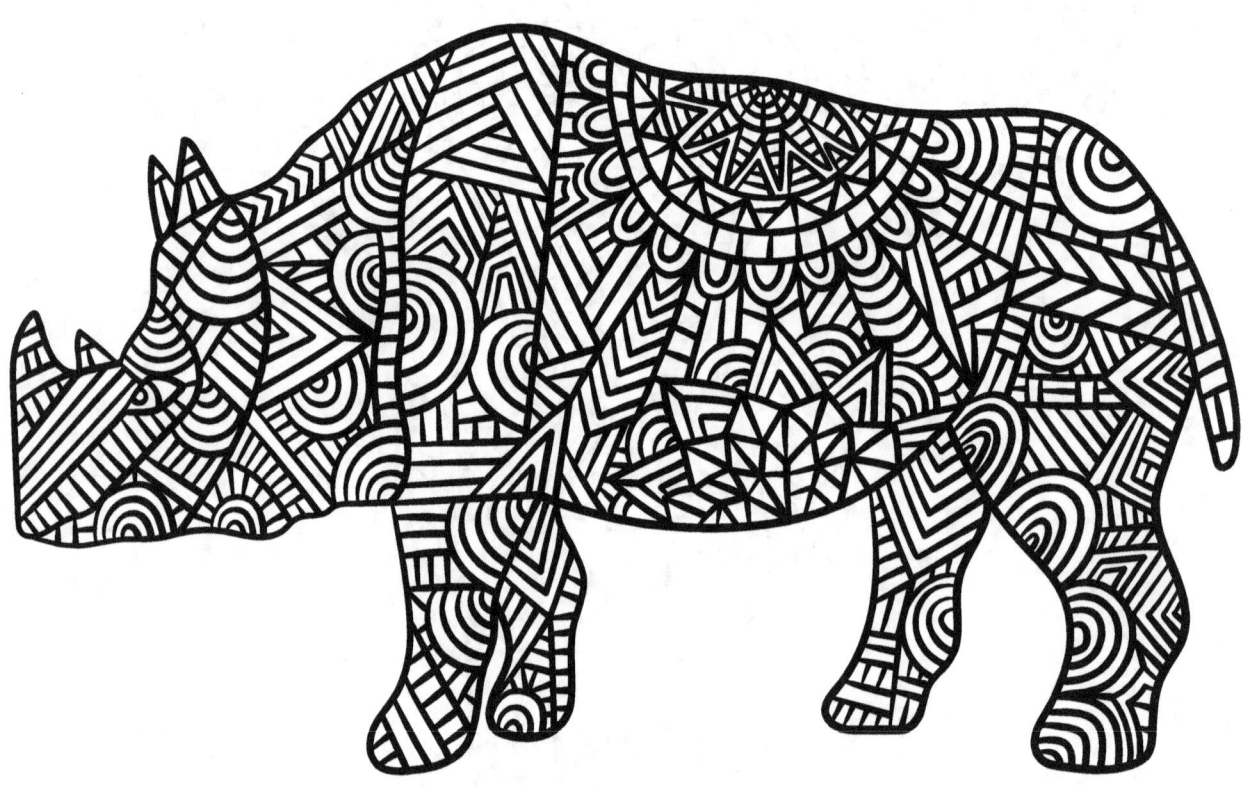

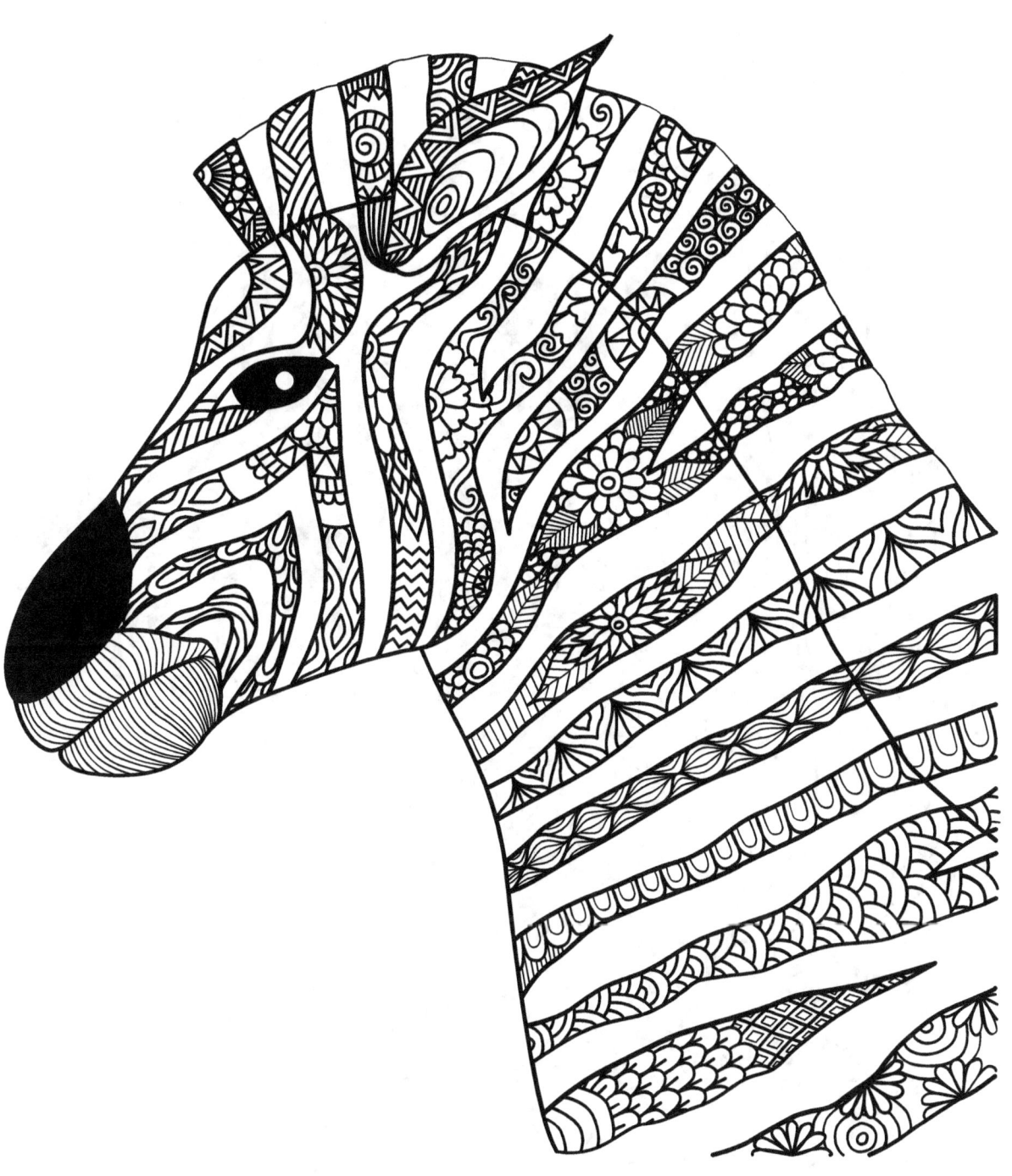

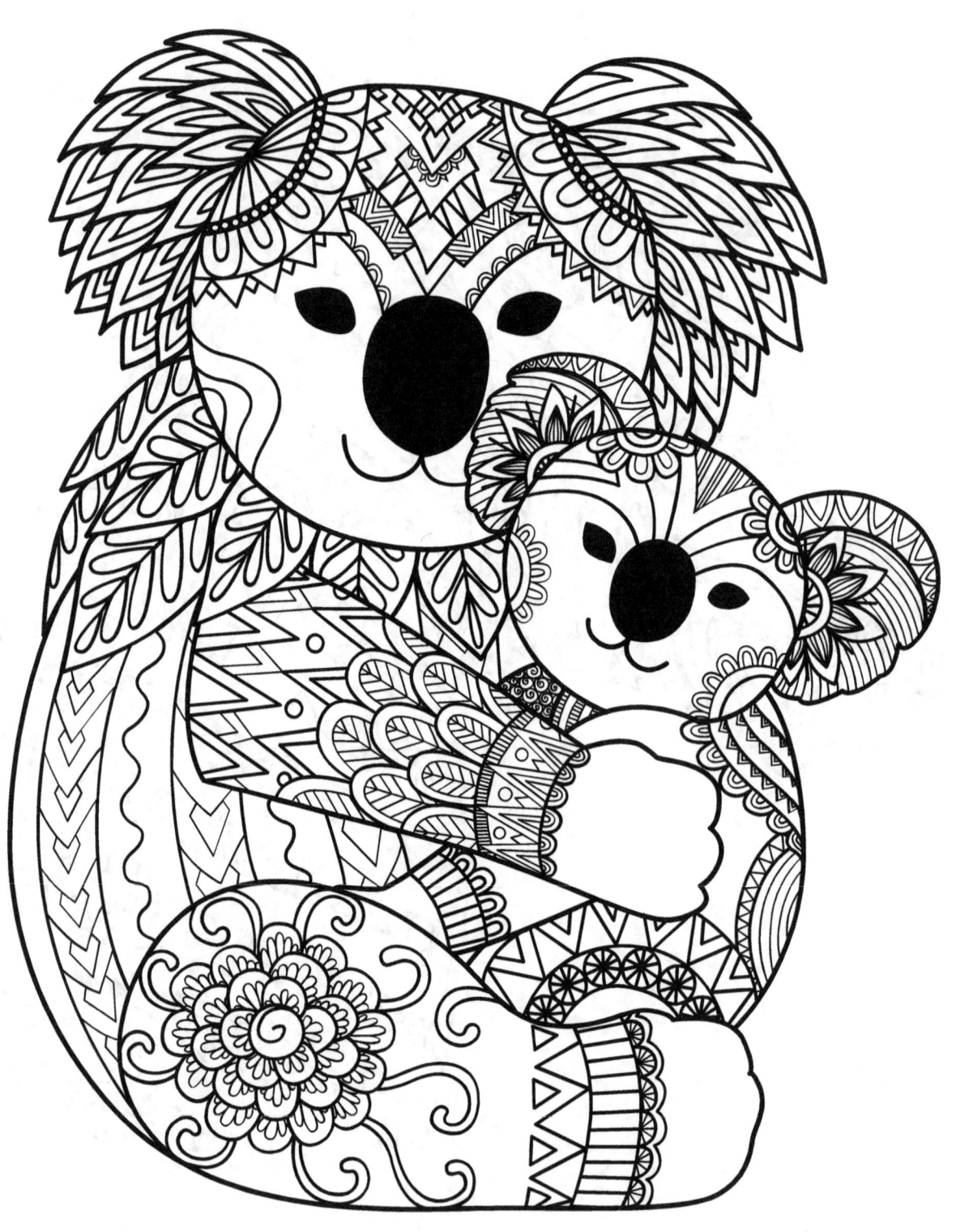

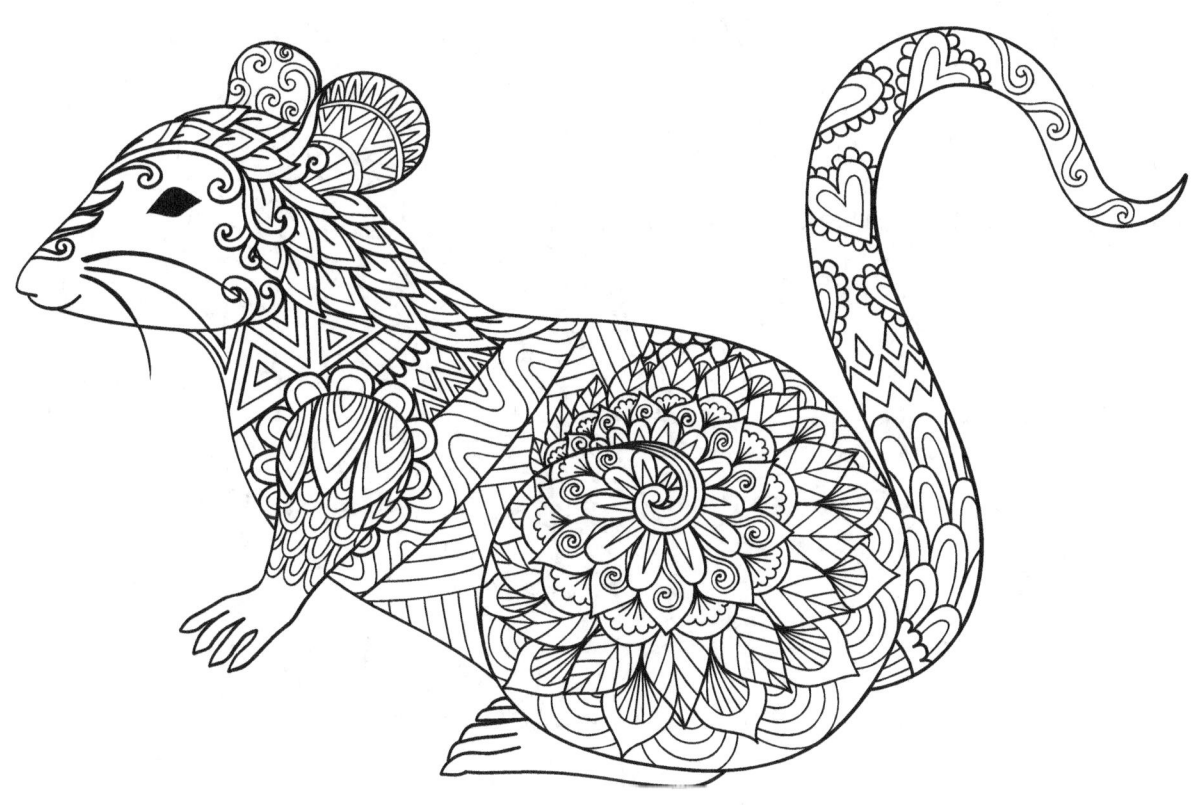

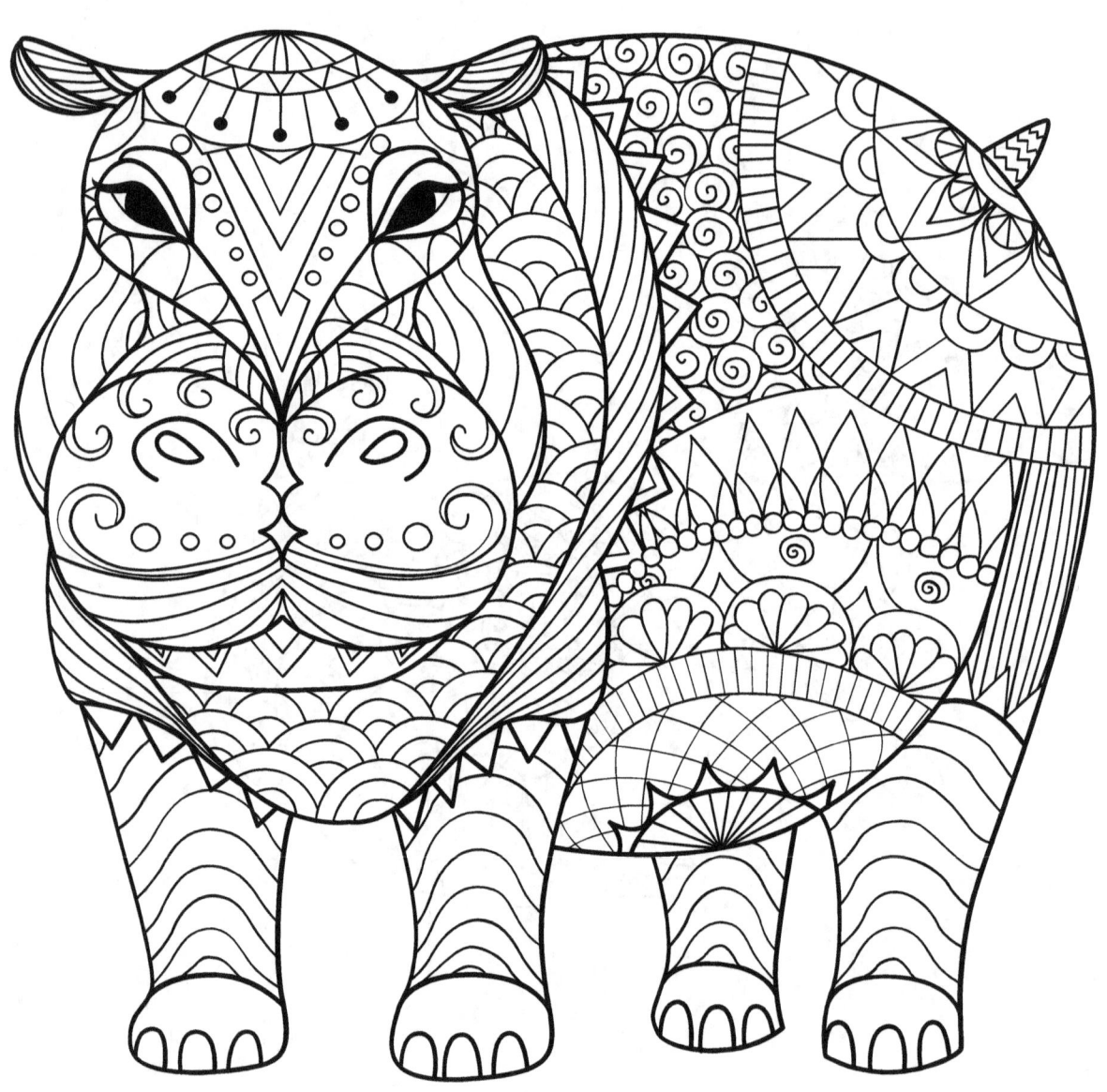

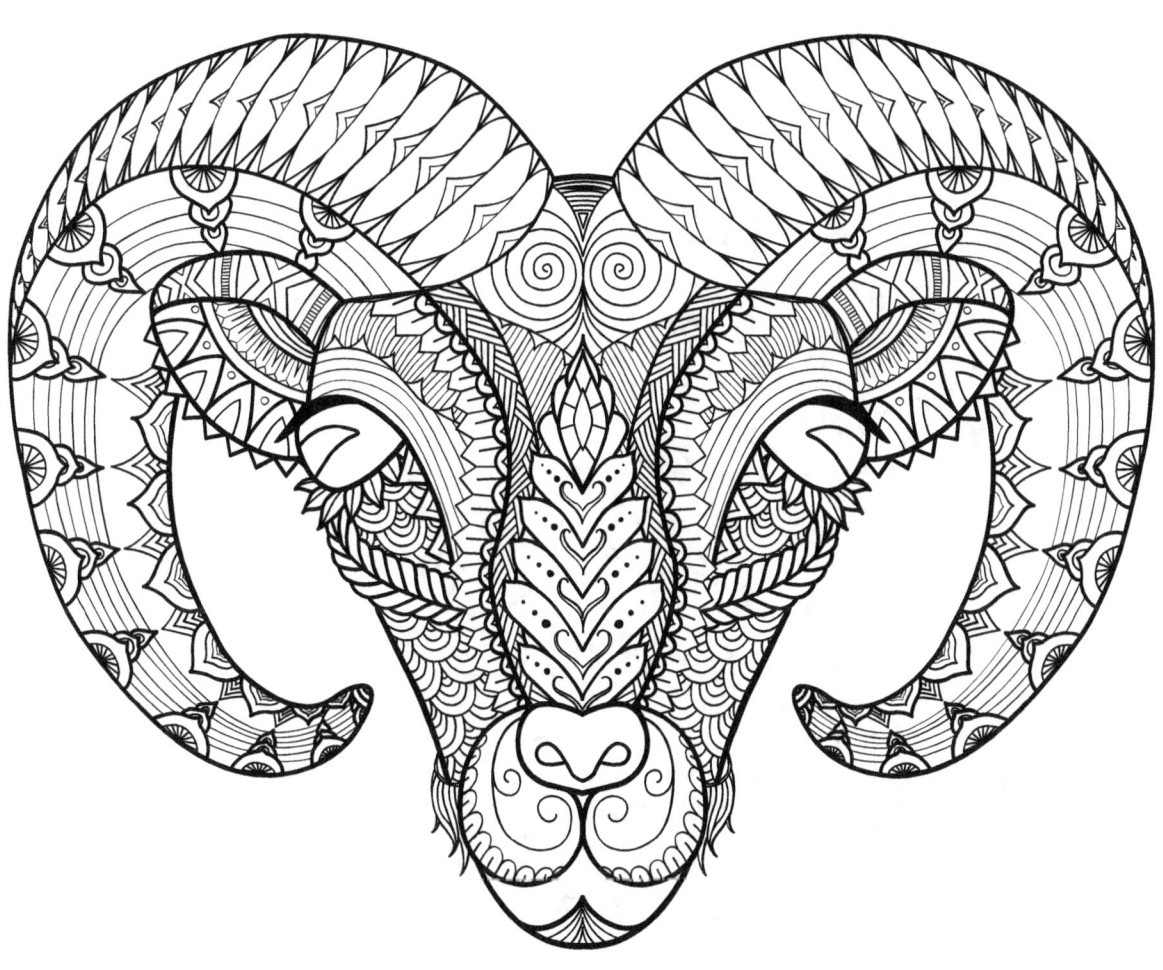

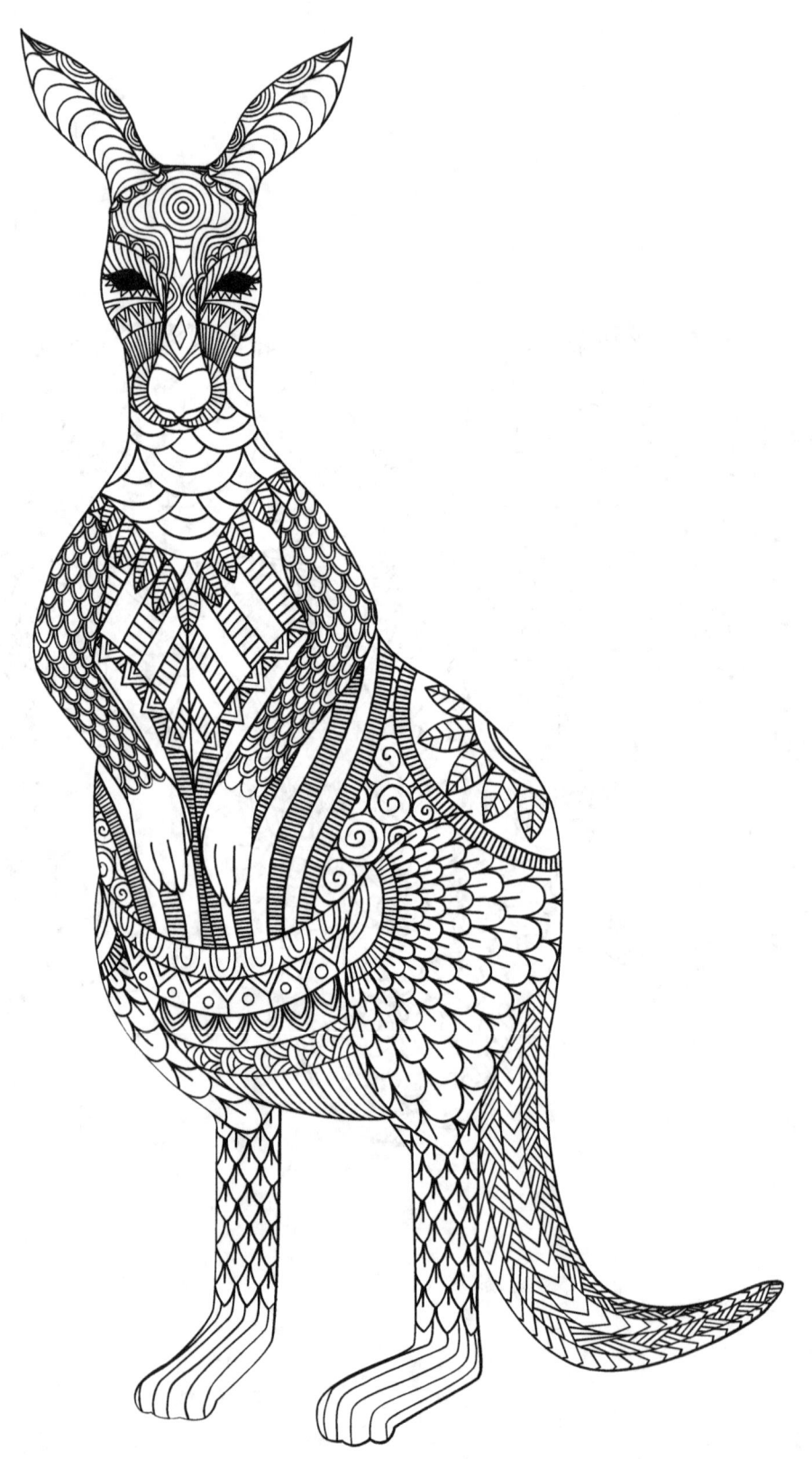

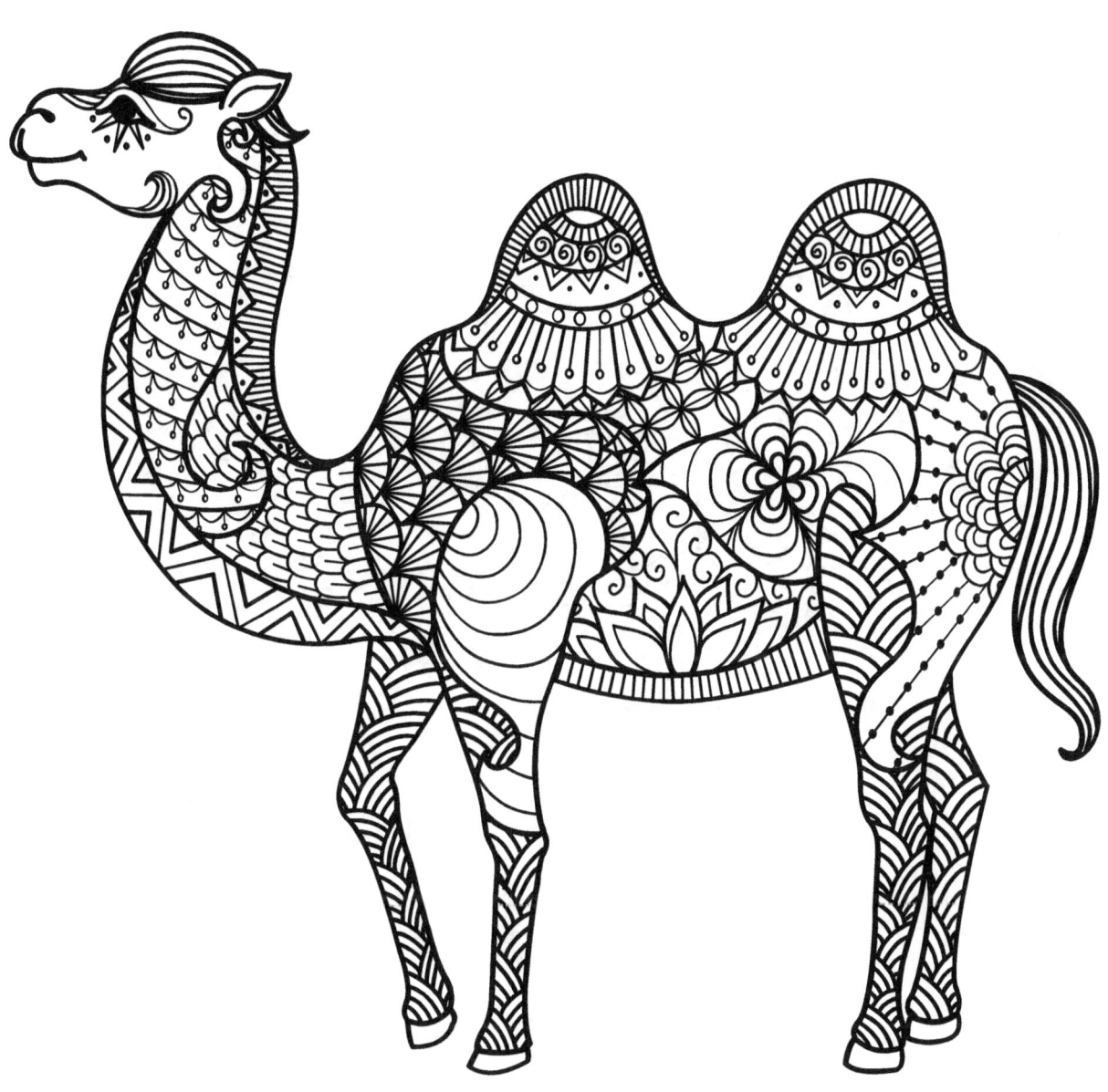

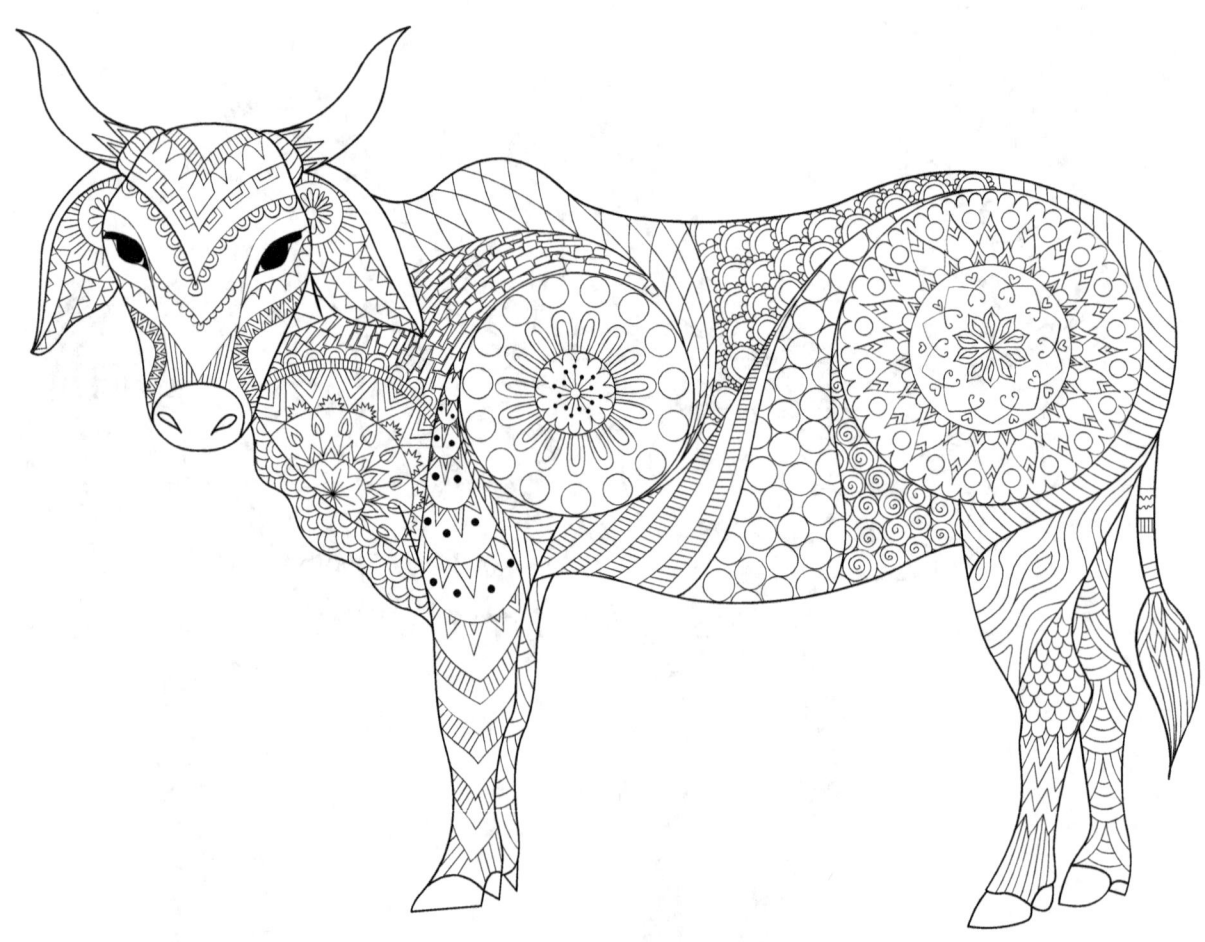

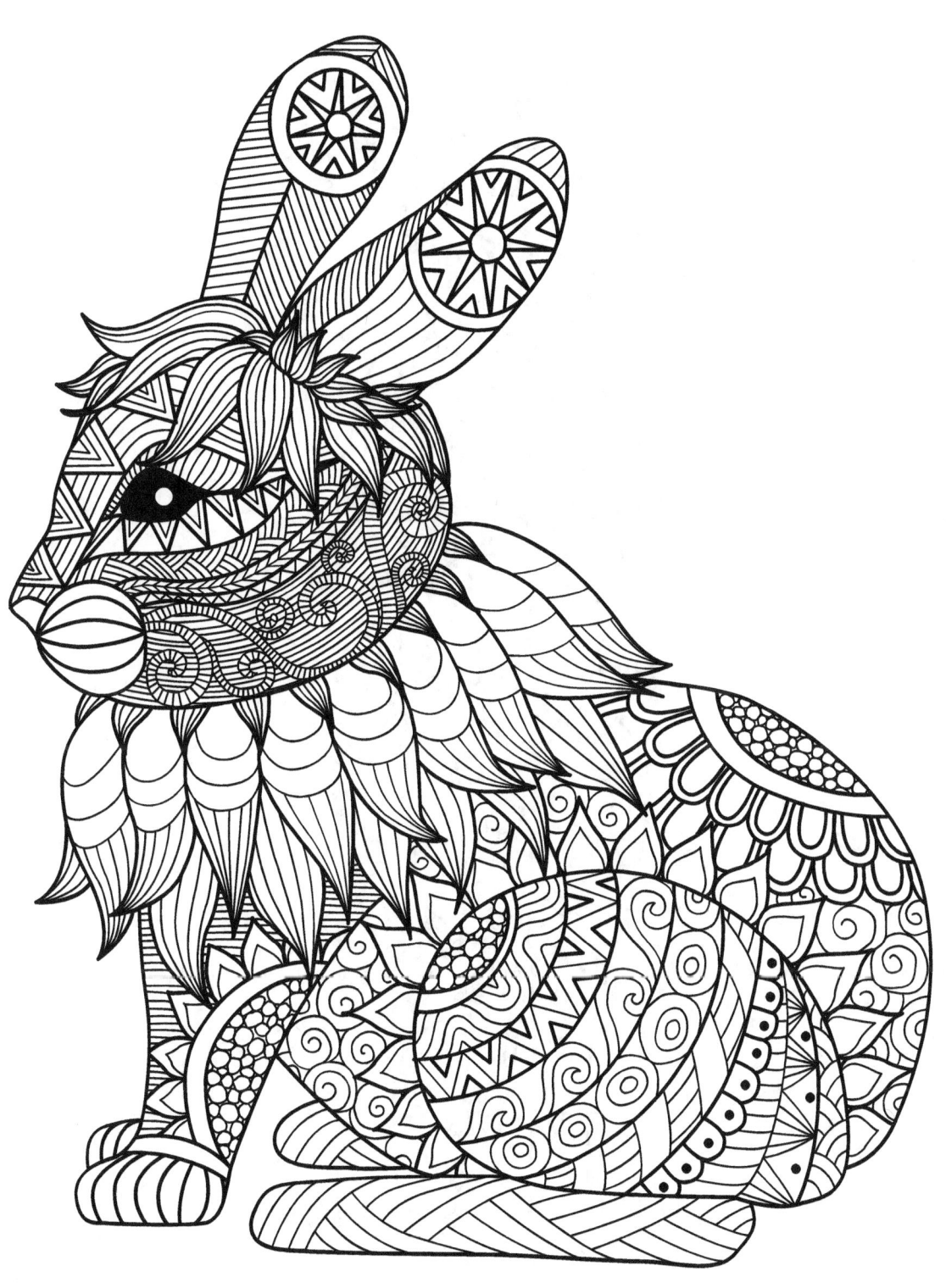

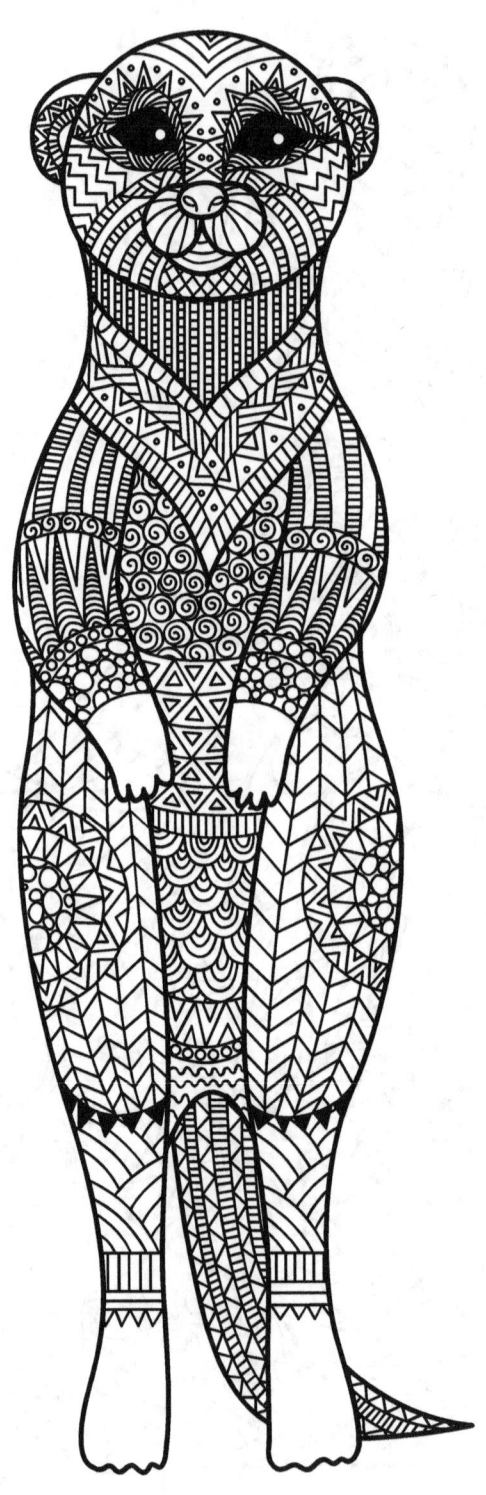

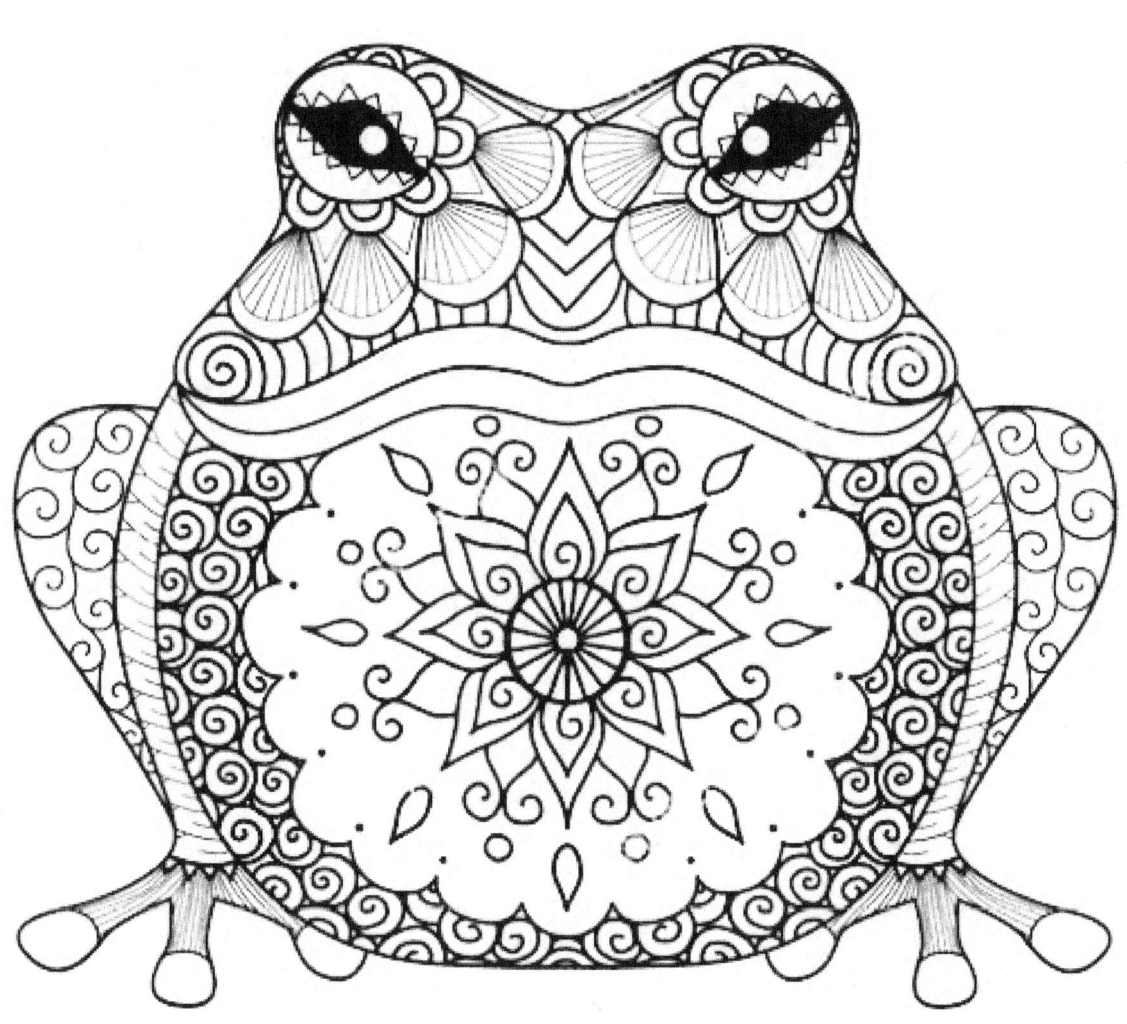

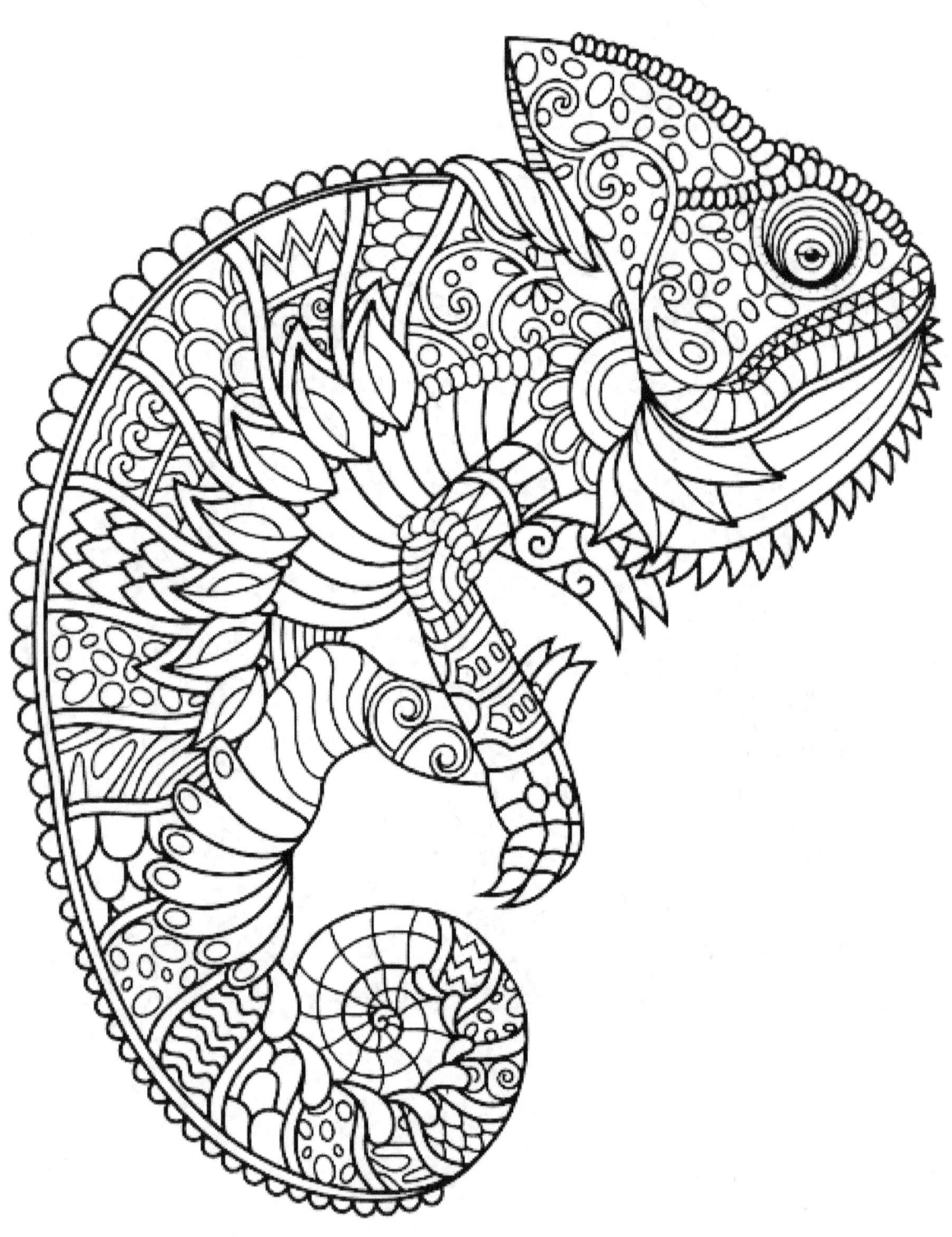

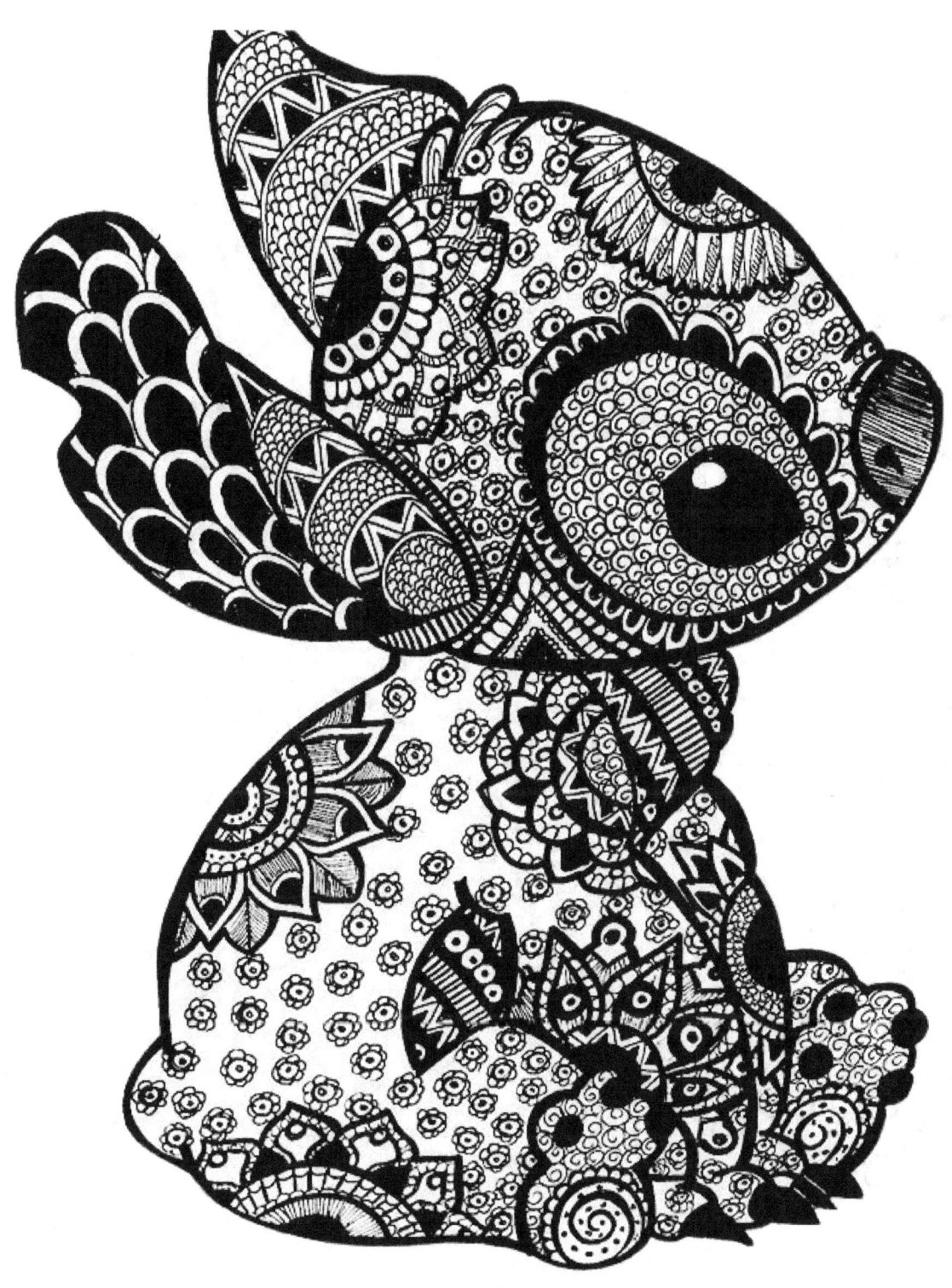

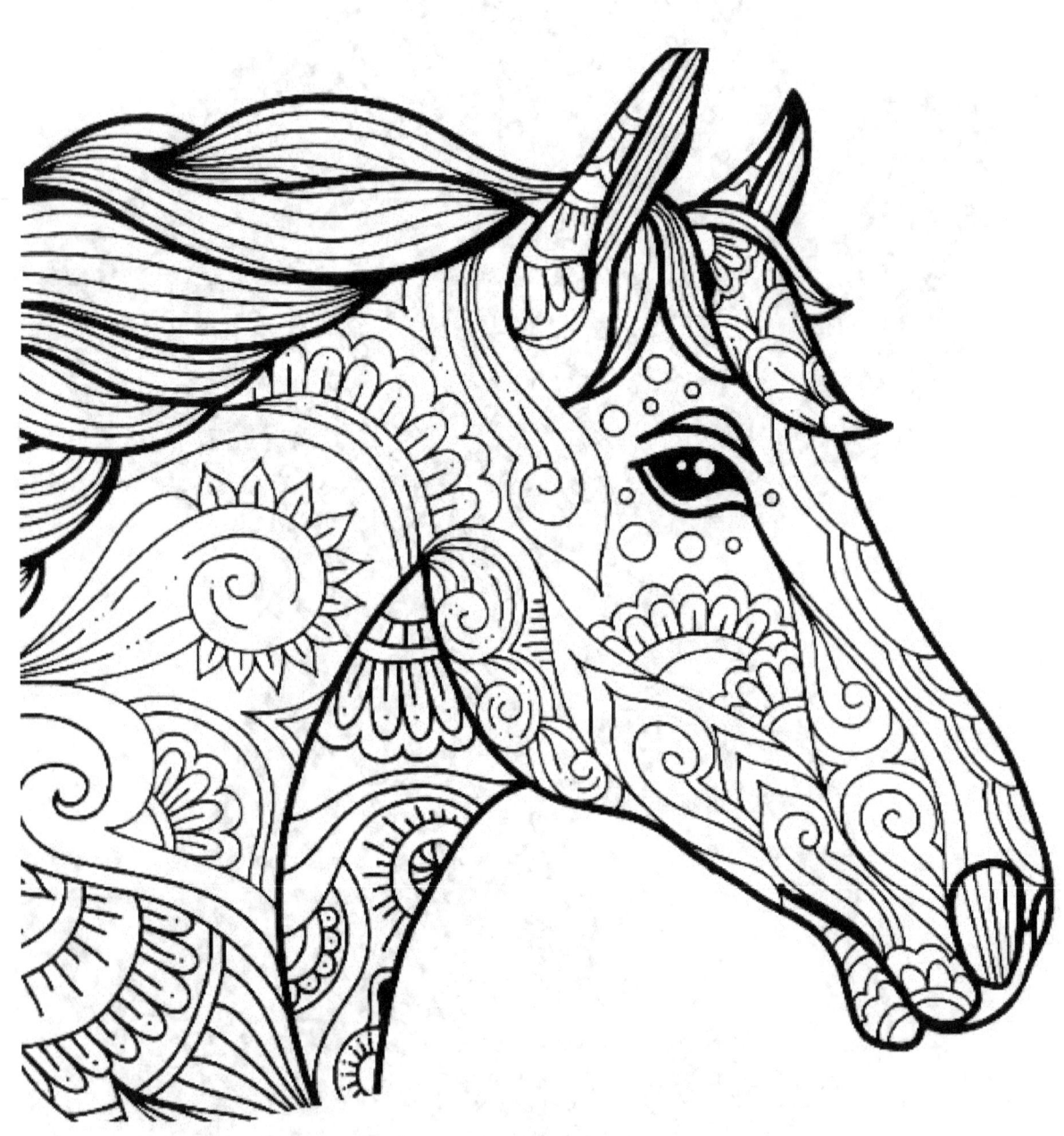

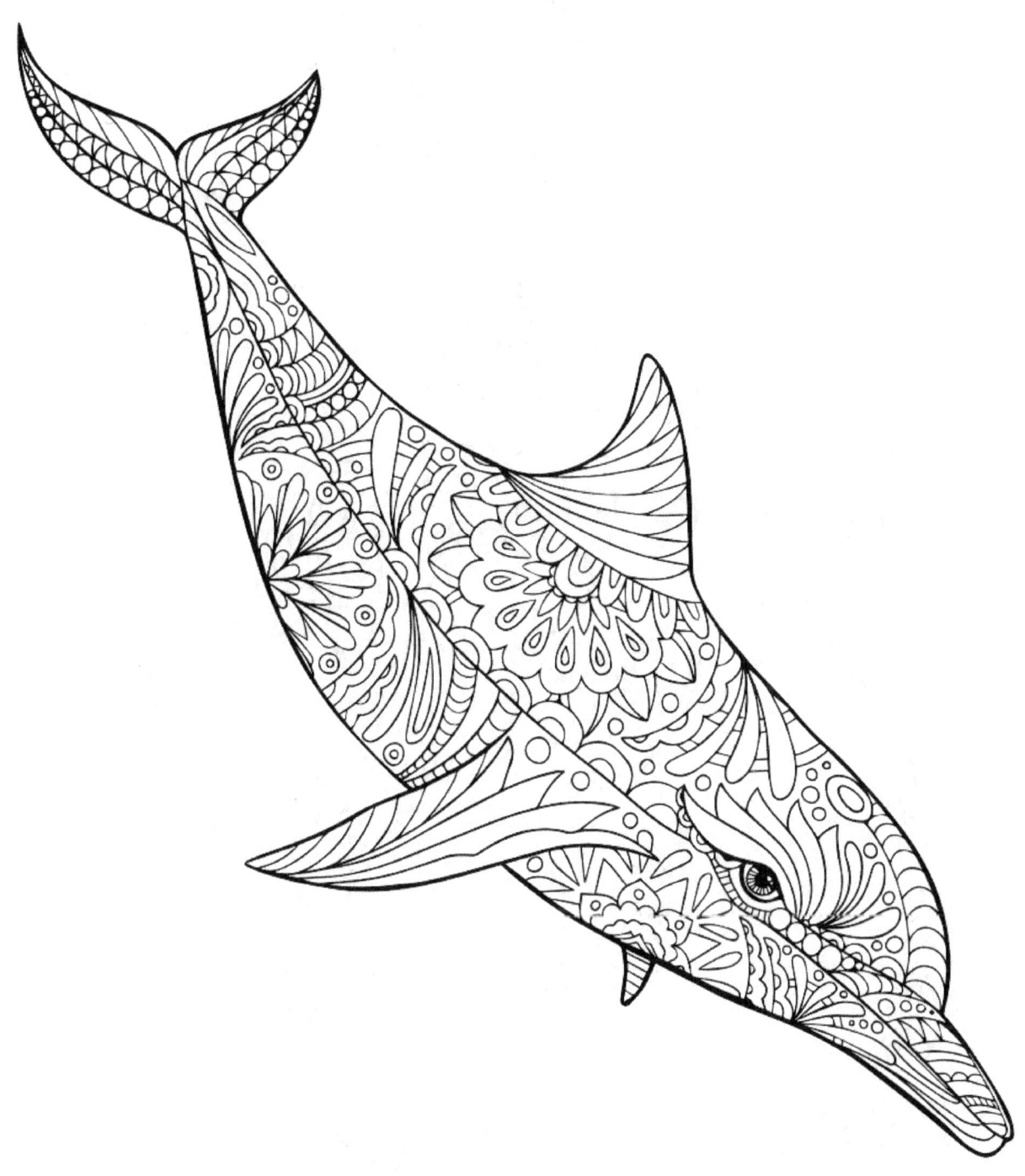

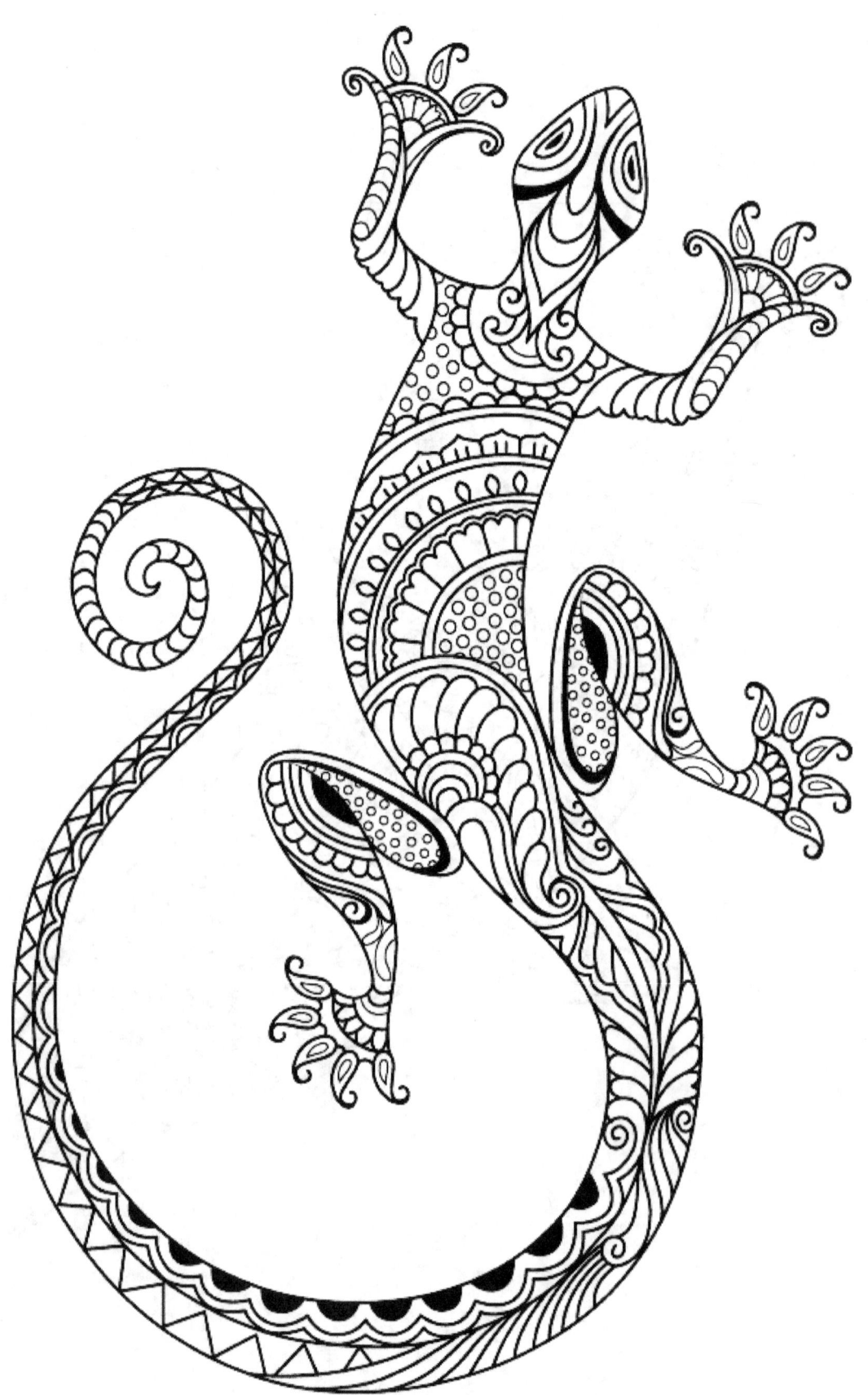

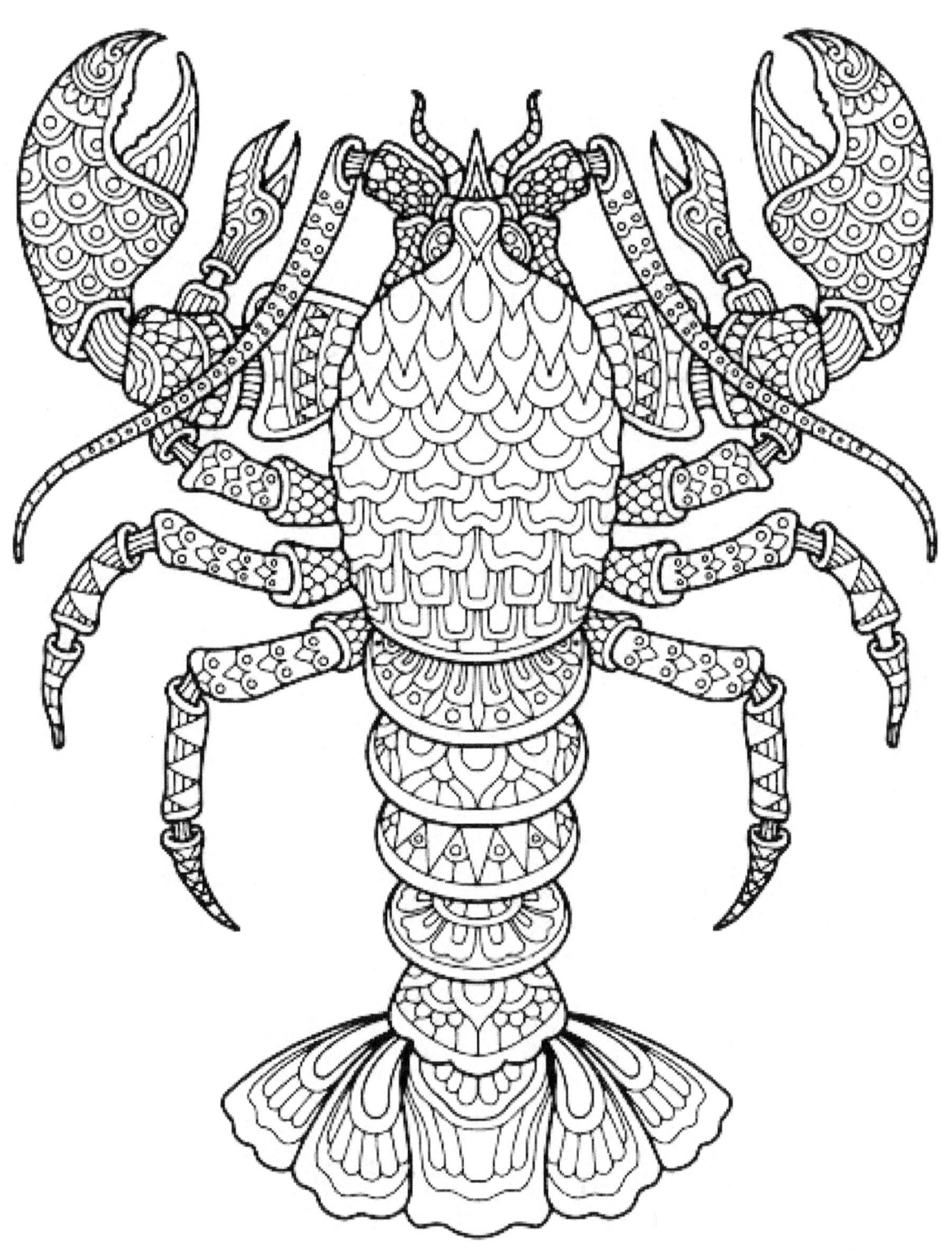

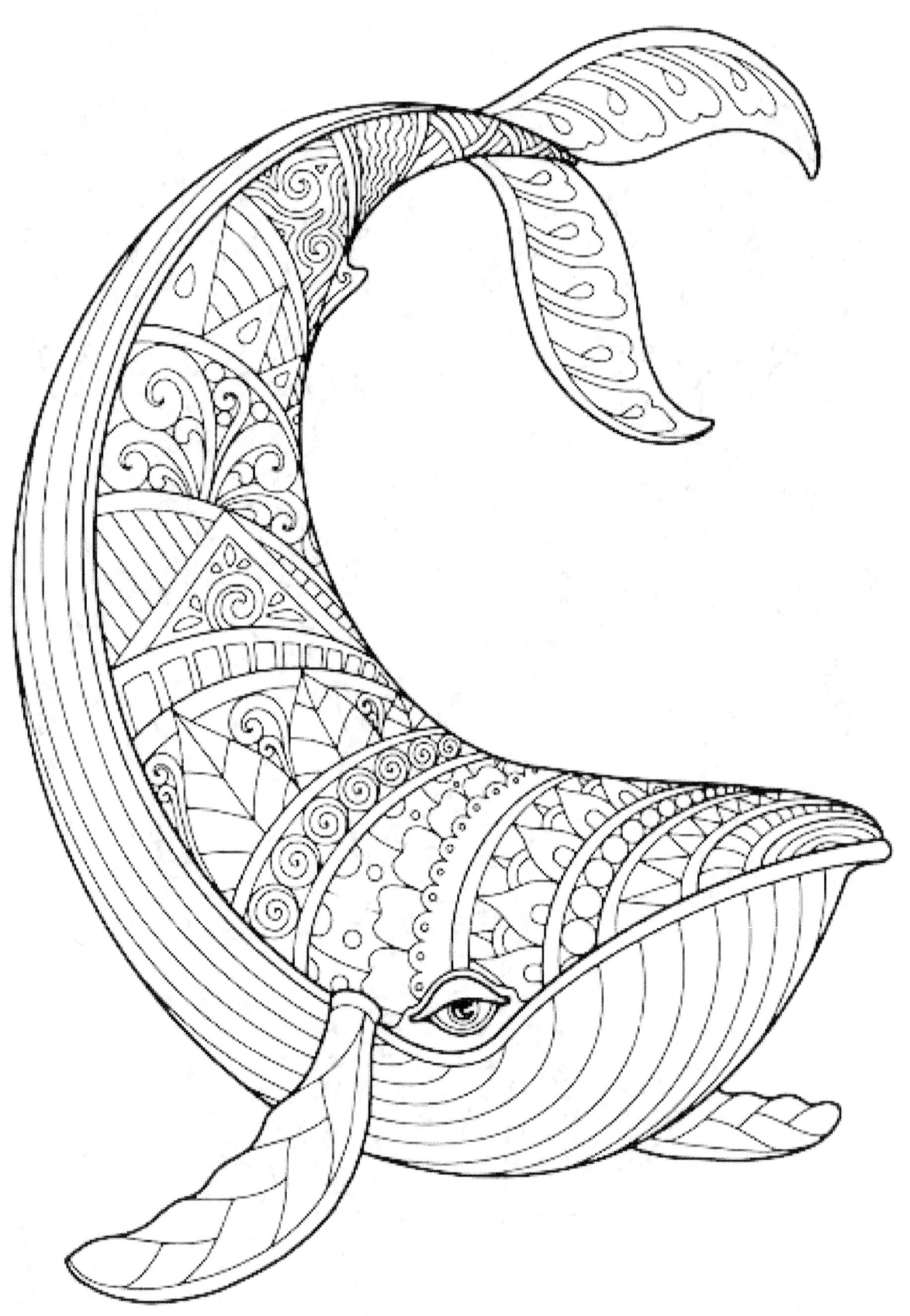

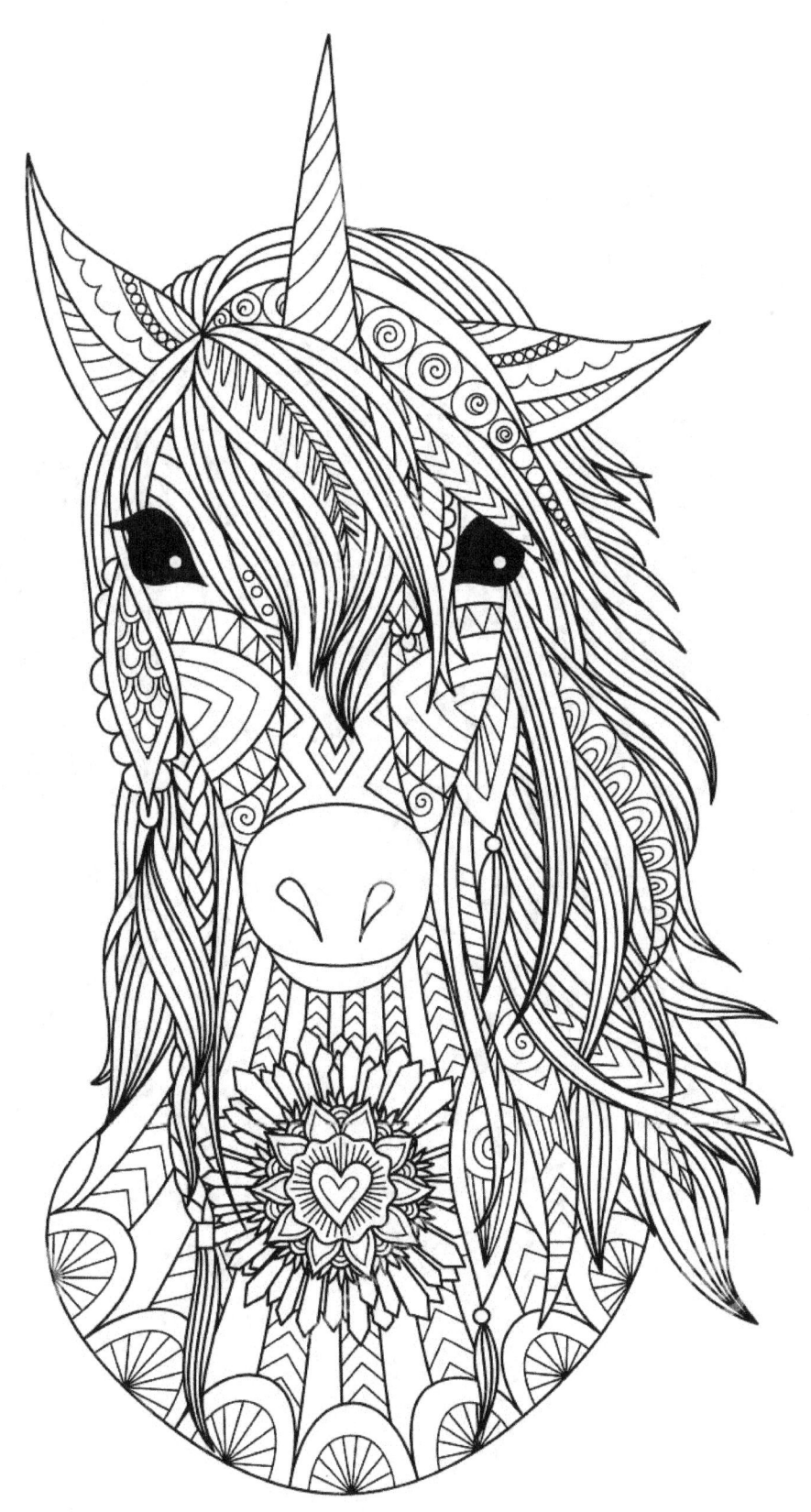

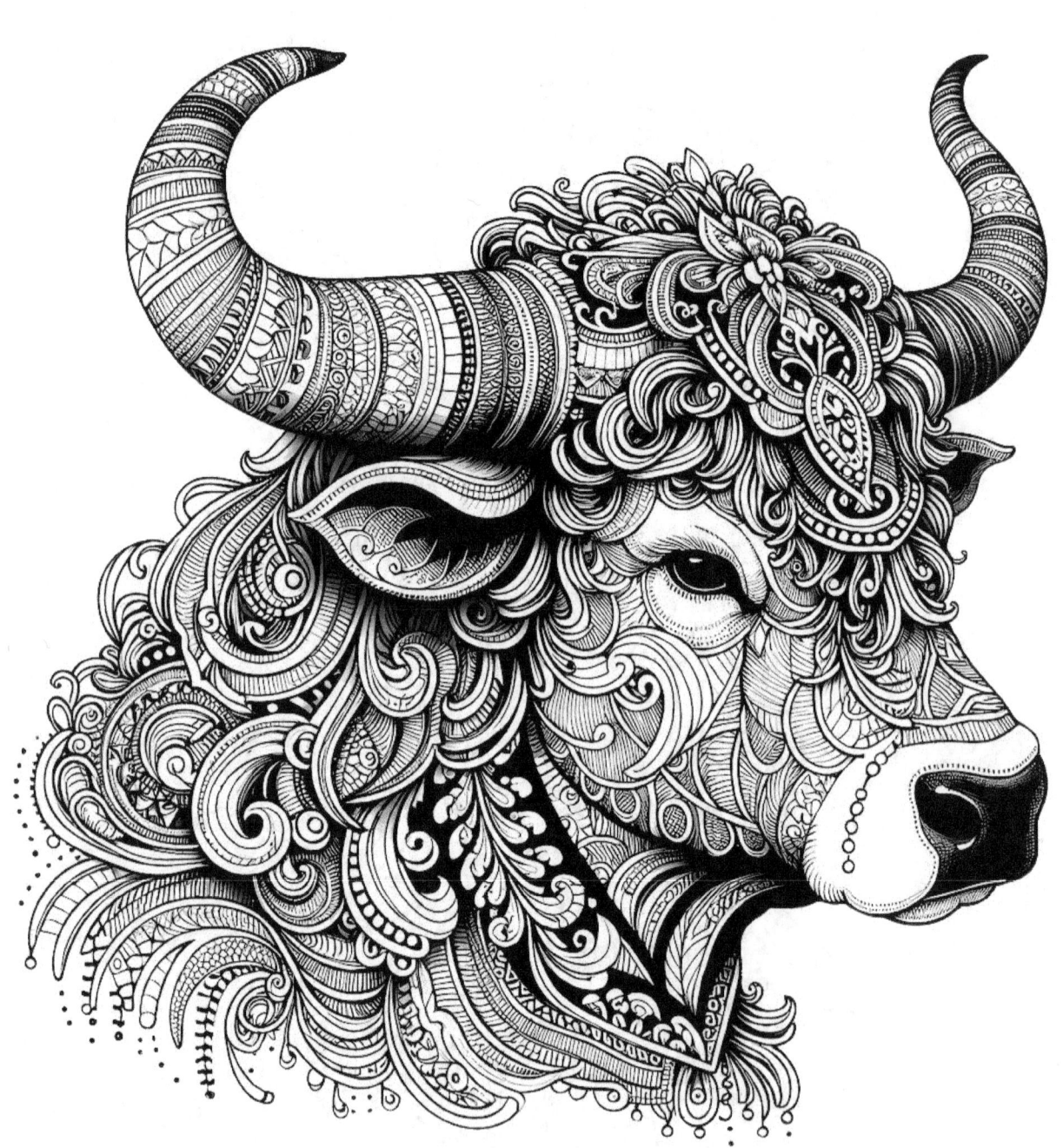

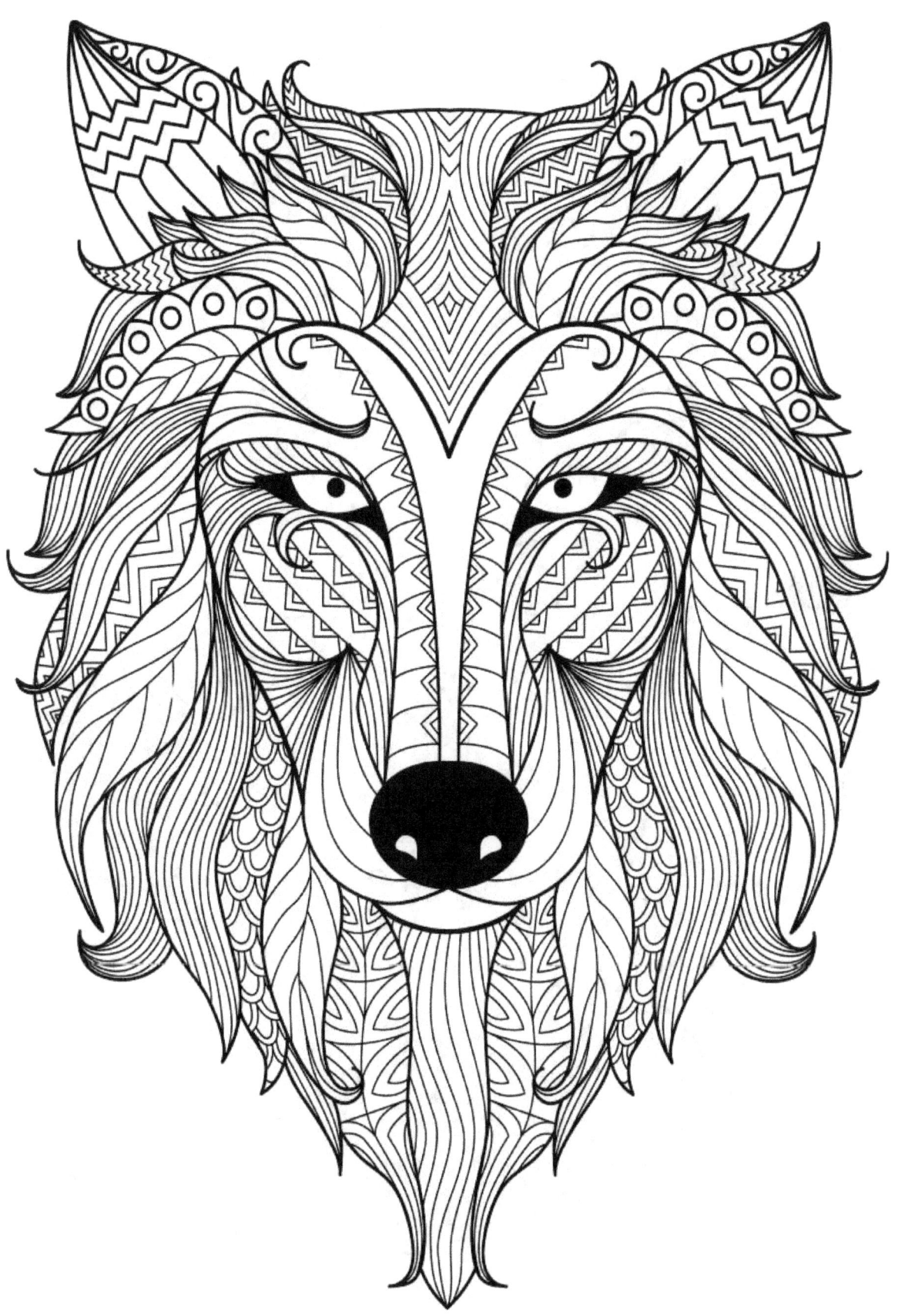

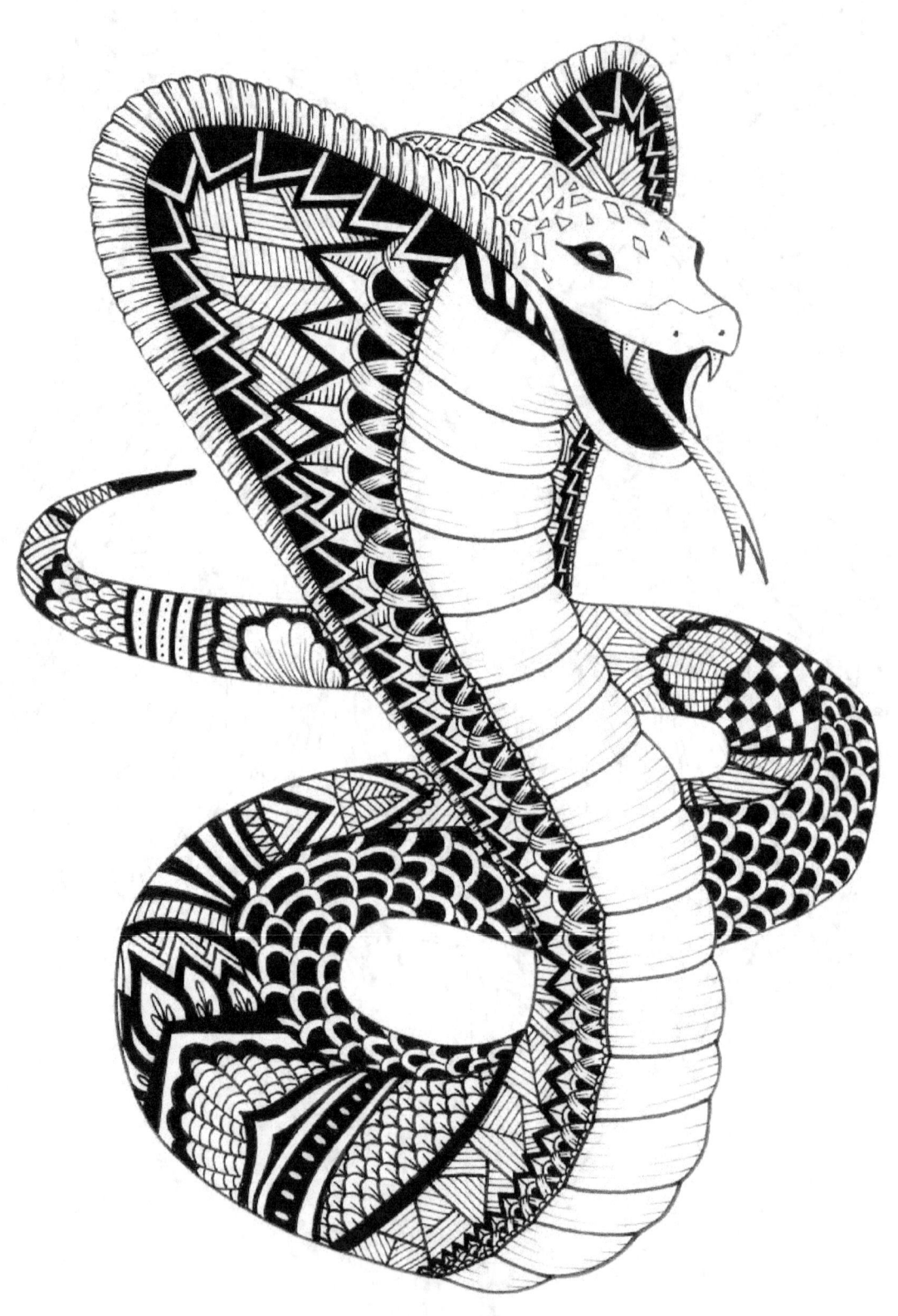

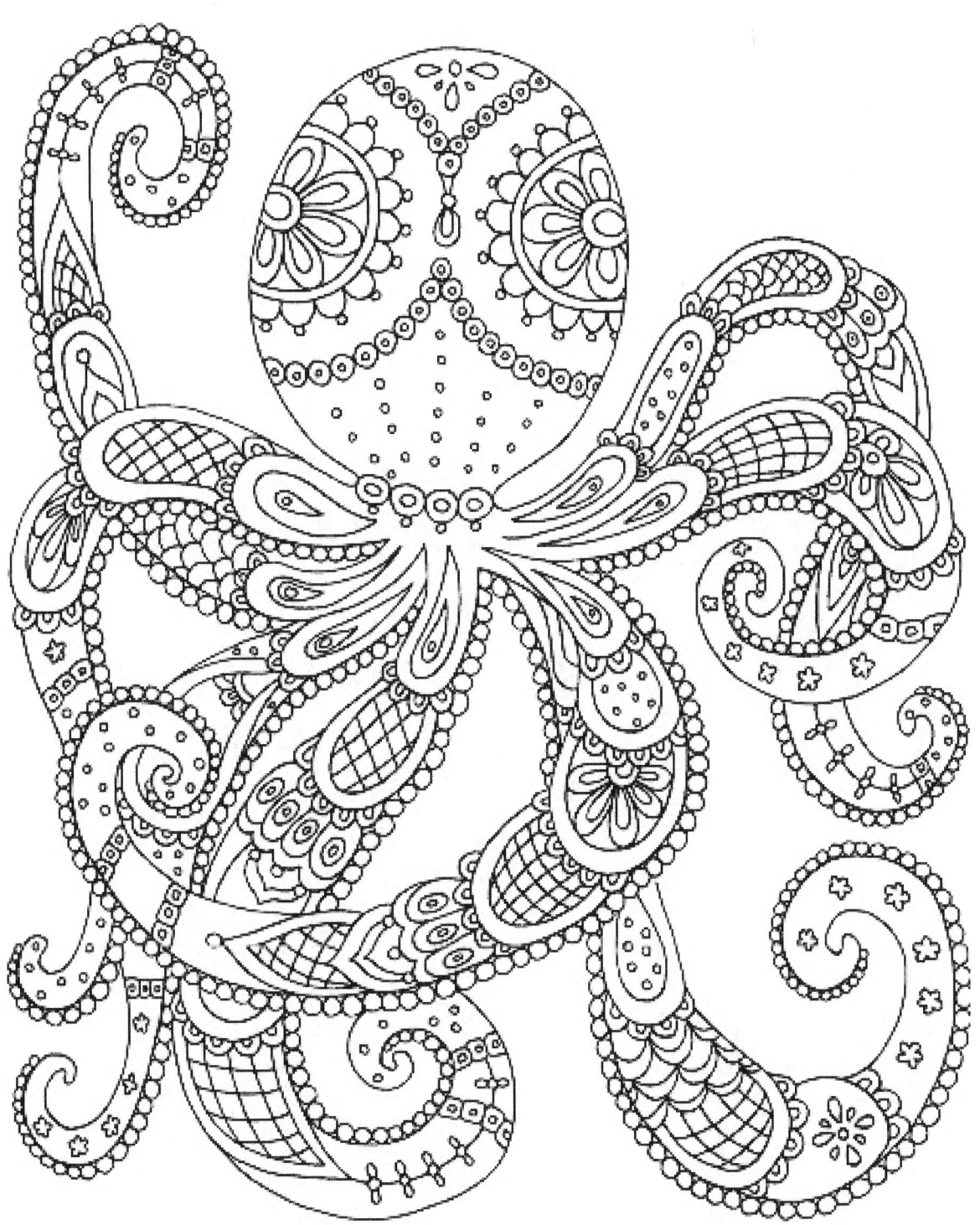

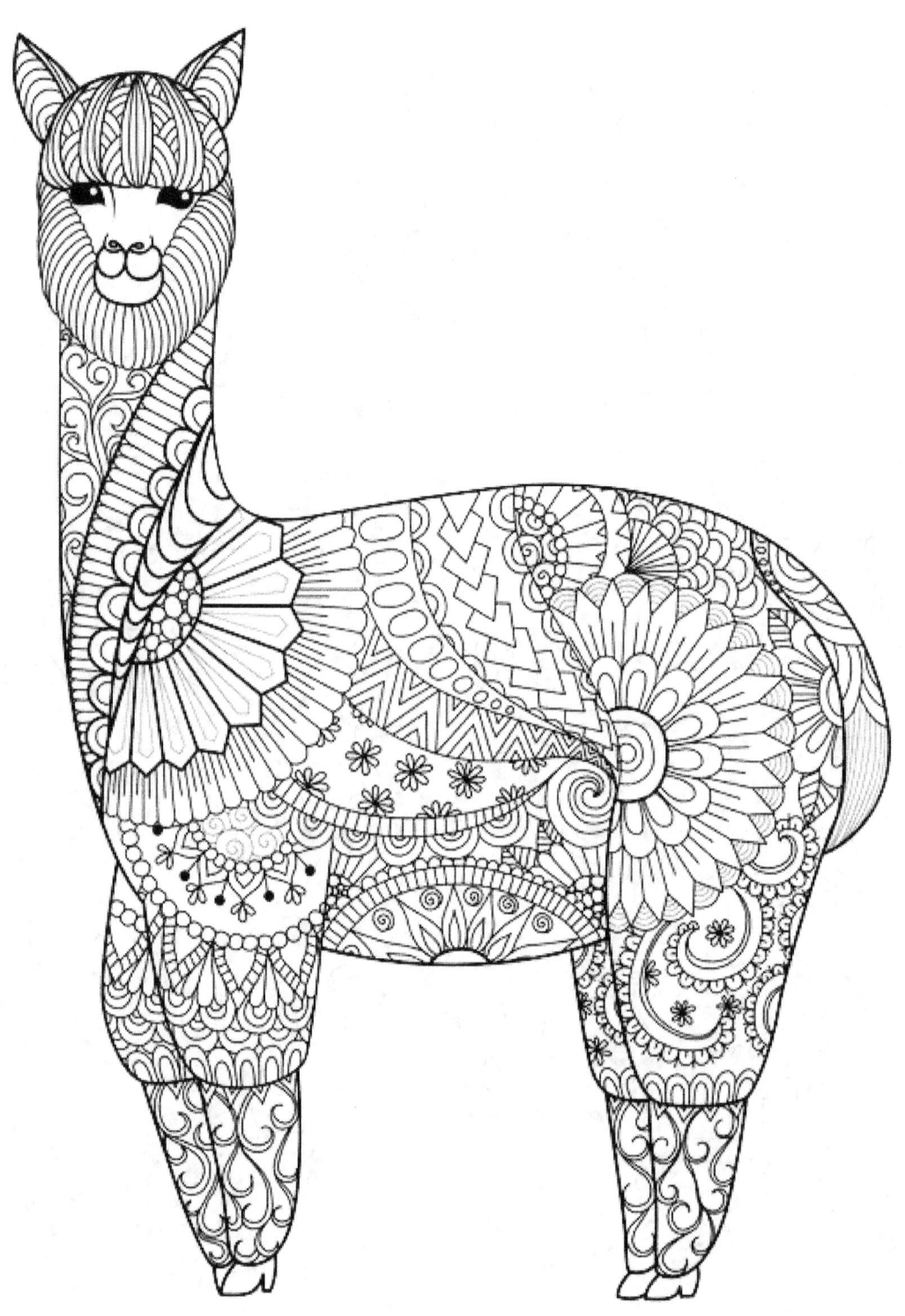

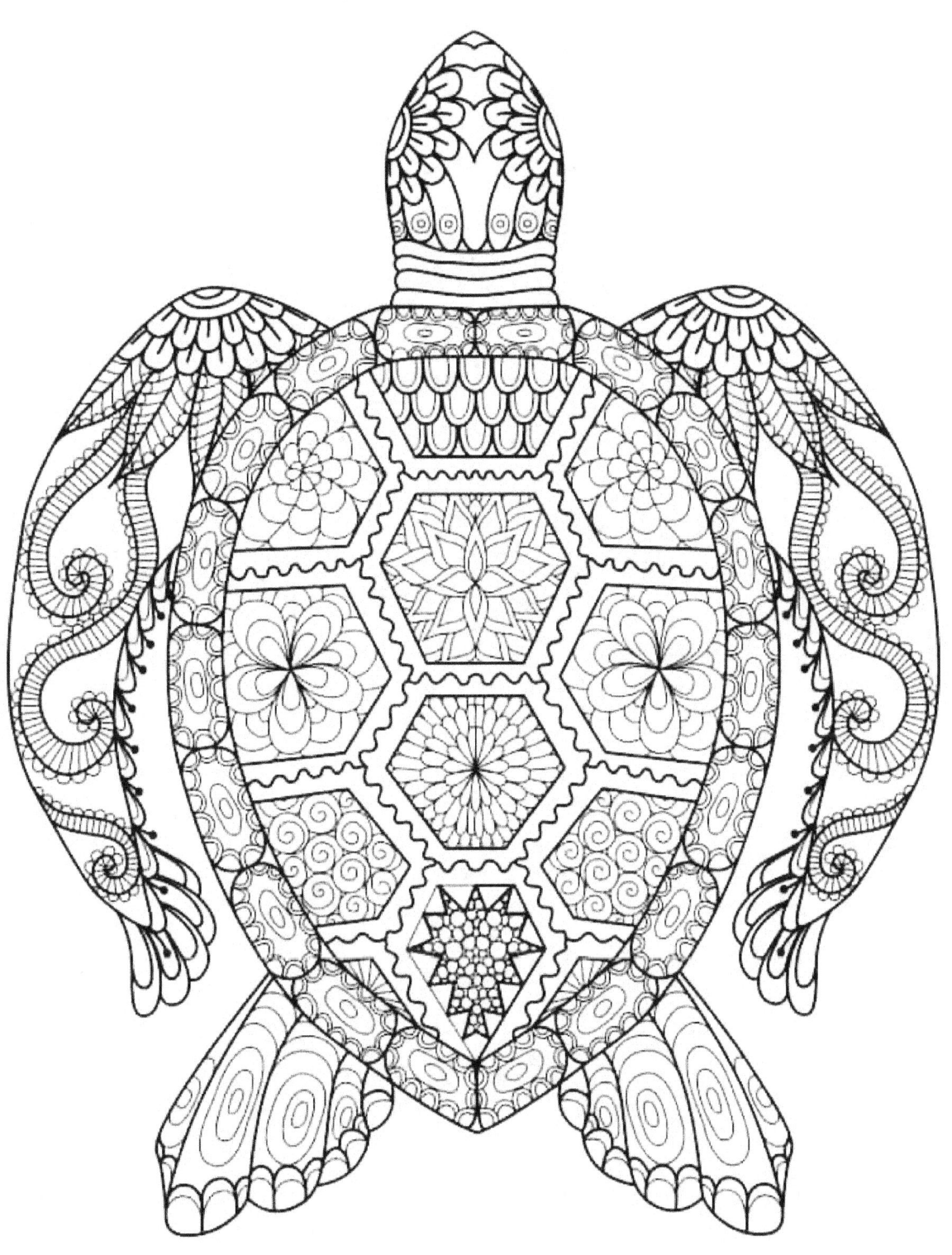

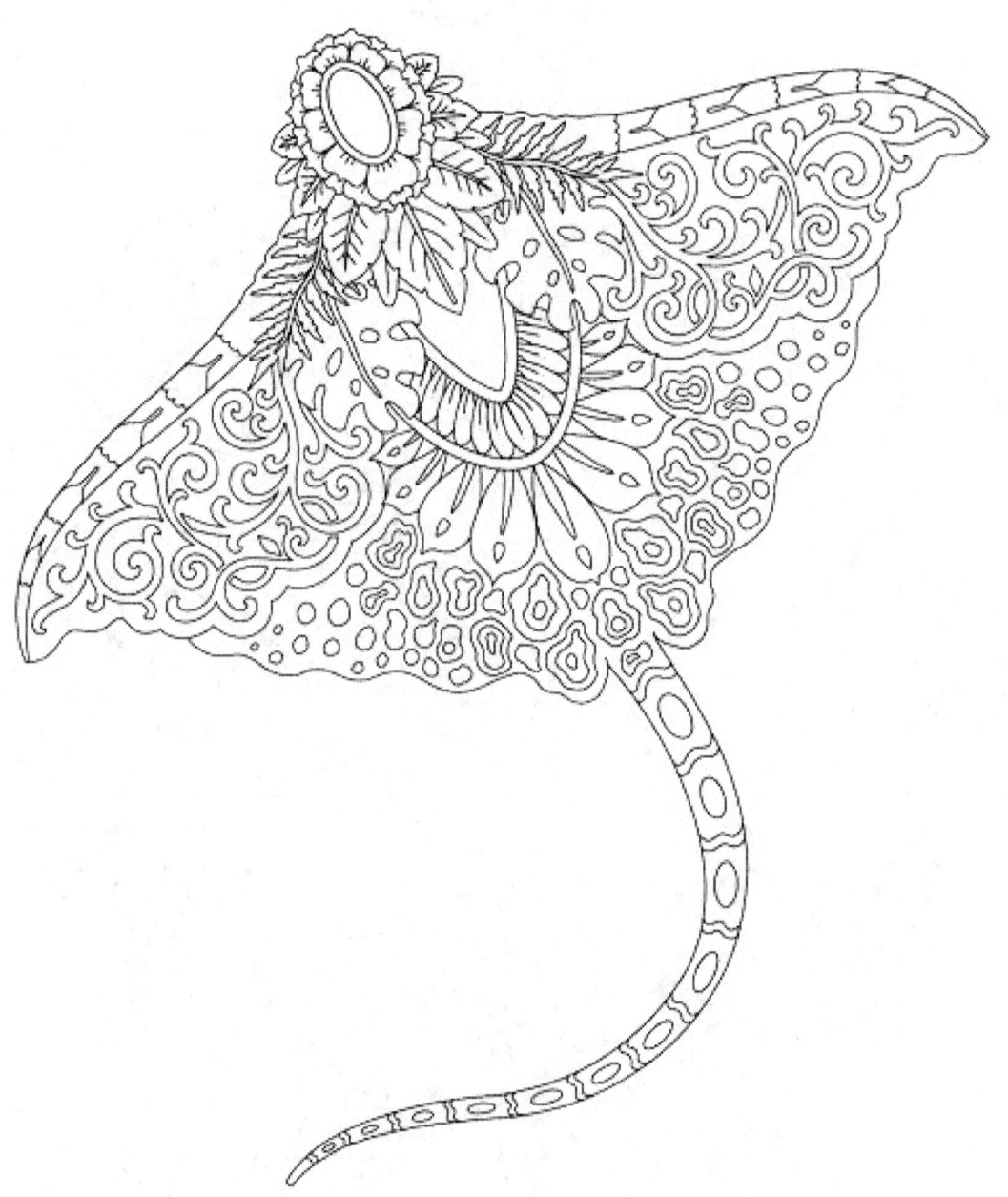

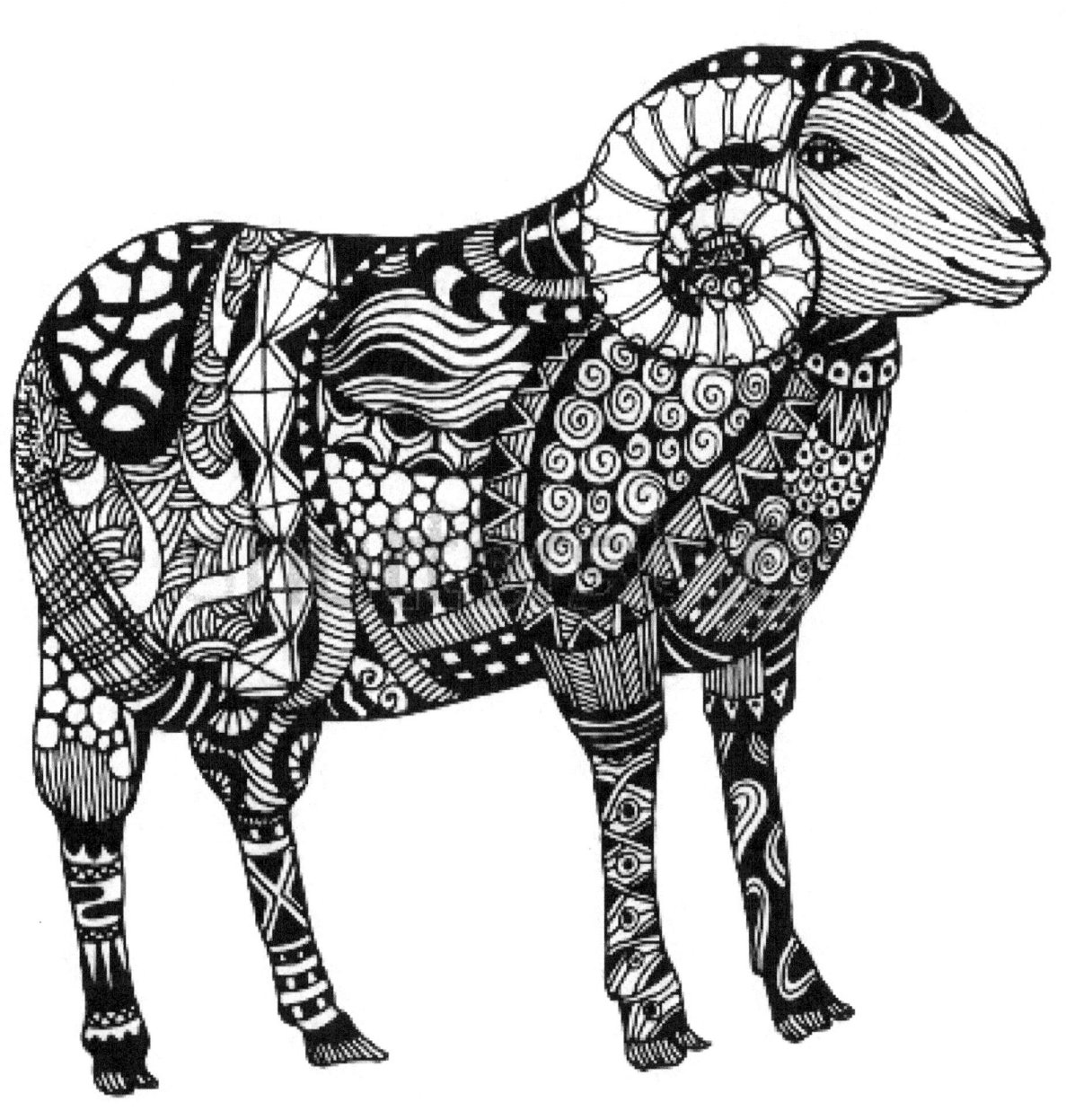

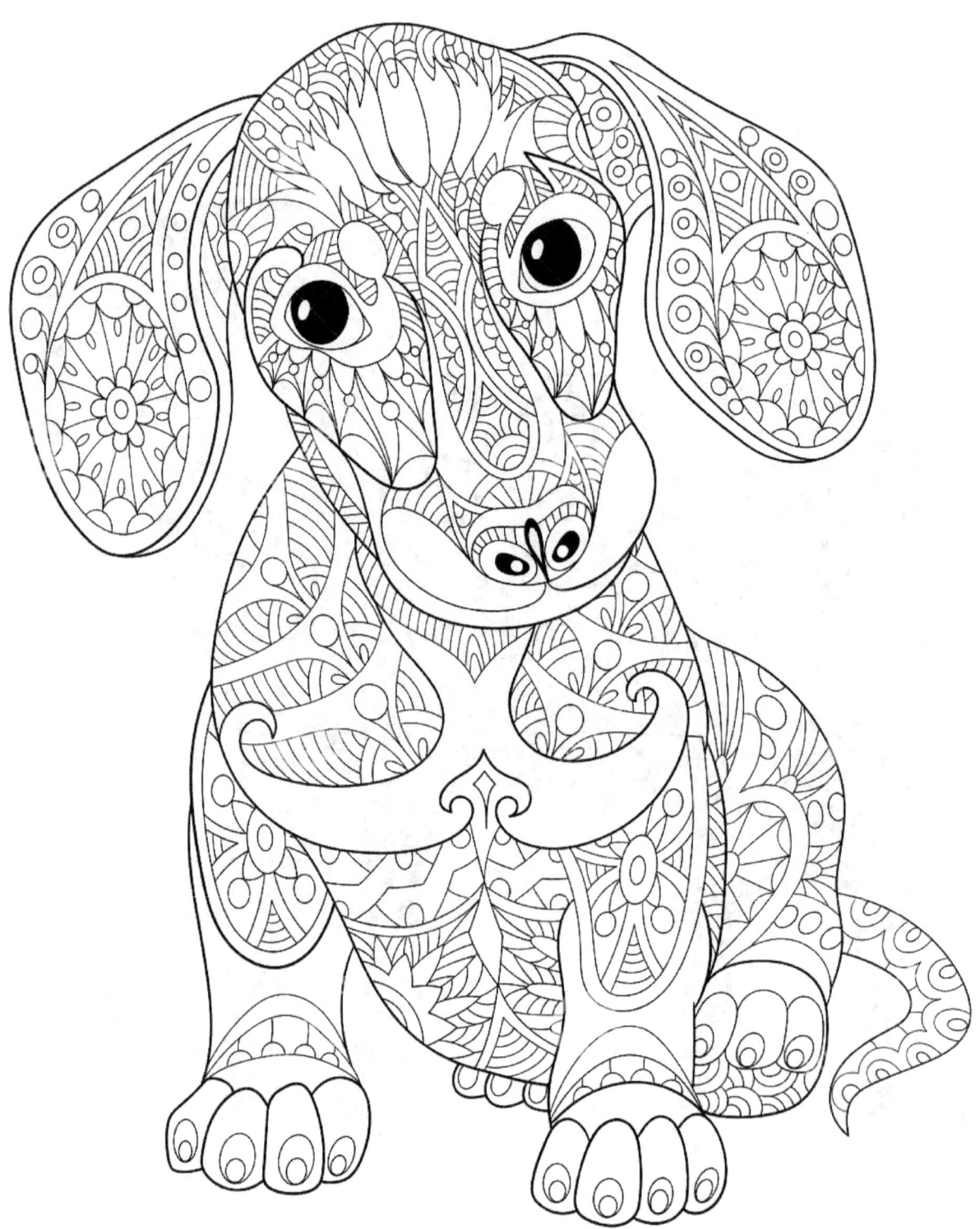

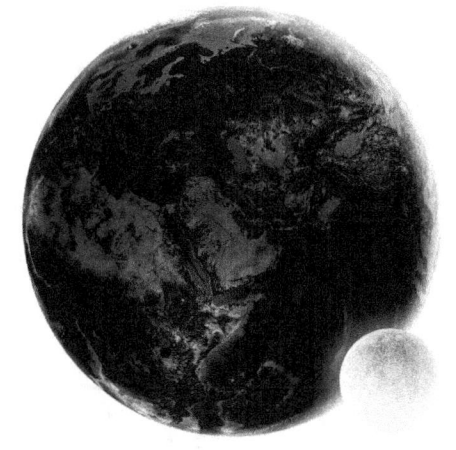
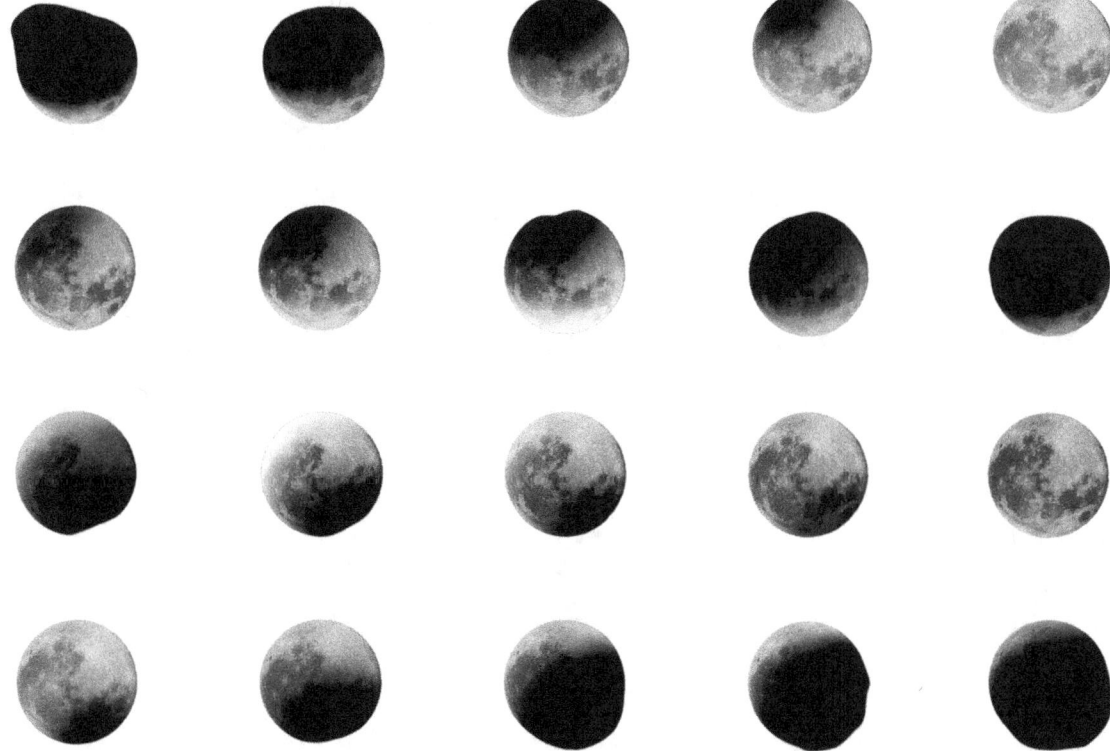

www.ingramcontent.com/pod-product-compliance
Lightning Source LLC
Chambersburg PA
CBHW062235220526
45471CB00009B/3484